PRIME-TIME FAMILIES

PRIME-TIME FAMILIES

Television Culture in Postwar America

ELLA TAYLOR

UNIVERSITY OF CALIFORNIA PRESS
BERKELEY   LOS ANGELES   LONDON

University of California Press
Berkeley and Los Angeles, California

University of California Press, Ltd.
London, England

© 1989 by
The Regents of the University of California

Library of Congress Cataloging-in-Publication Data

Taylor, Ella.
    Prime-time families : television culture in postwar America/Ella
Taylor.
        p. cm.
        Based on the author's thesis (Brandeis University).
        Bibliography: p.
        Includes index.
        ISBN 0-520-05867-4 (alk. paper)
        1. Television and family—United States.   2. Television serials—
United States.   I. Title.
    PN1992.8.F33T39   1990
    302.23′45′0973 — dc20

                                                                        89-31544
                                                                        CIP

Printed in the United States of America
1   2   3   4   5   6   7   8   9

For my parents,
Hannah and Sol Gafan,
who, by creating quiet time and space
in which to do homework,
turned their daughter into an intellectual

Contents

Tables

Acknowledgments

Successive drafts of this book have trotted obediently about the United States with me as I made the transition from graduate student to assistant professor. As a result I have received more help and support with this project than it takes to make a miniseries. At Brandeis University, Maurice Stein, Egon Bittner, Kurt Wolff, and George Ross provided insight and encouragement in unlimited quantities, along with a willingness to have the boundaries of sociology stretched to meet the requirements of an interdisciplinary study. The final shape of this book owes a great deal to the formidable critical intelligence of Michael Rogin, my unseen reviewer at the University of California at Berkeley, who commented extensively on two versions. Two anonymous reviewers made suggestions that greatly eased the work of revision.

In Boston, Andrea Walsh brought her prodigious knowledge of film and television to bear on successive drafts of the manuscript. Joel Greifinger was my first guide through the labyrinth of American television history. His erudition in cultural theory and television studies have influenced my work enormously, as has the combination of intellectual agility, wicked wit, and grace with which he habitually encouraged me to sharpen my thoughts. "So," he observed genially as I expounded my theory of realism in television, "what you're trying to say is that people think that *Fantasy Island* is a documentary?"

Lynn Davidman, Robert Horwitz, Sonya Michel, Mitchell Silver, and Carmen Sirianni commented on substantial portions of the manuscript in detail. Art Goldhammer in Boston and John Bowes and Pat Dinning in Seattle spent hours at various stages coaxing my intransigent software into producing final copies. Lee Biggerstaff showed unvarying good humor in the face of requests to type awkward portions of manuscript at short notice. Sarah Key provided invaluable research assistance during my stay at the Annenberg School of Communications at the University of Southern California in Los Angeles.

Numerous others gave me intellectual and moral support, as well as dinner when things got hectic—in particular Allan Arkush, Harriet Baxter, Susan Biskeborn, Wini Breines, Mary Bruno, Anita Diamant, Stephanie Engel, Ora Gladstone, Herman Gray, Judy Howard, Cheryl Klausner, Lynne Layton, Netta Rice, Michal Safdie, George Scialabba, Ann Senechal, and Svi Shapiro. Evan Watkins suggested a change that liberated me from one of those stuck positions that are the occupational hazard of writers. My colleagues in the School of Communications at the University of Washington created time and a supportive environment in which to finish this project. Students who took my media courses at Brandeis, Clark University, Northeastern University, the Annenberg School, and the University of Washington kept me on my toes with their knowledge and enthusiasm and occasionally by dropping quietly off to sleep. Naomi Schneider, Steve Rice, and Marilyn Schwartz at the University of California Press advised and encouraged in countless ways. Richard Miller edited the manuscript with all the skill, tact, and restraint a writer could wish for in an editor.

While I was working on this book I also wrote regular television reviews for a number of papers. Sounding off in print about individual shows and current trends in television helped me to avoid an excess of careless generalizations and kept me honest. So did my editors, Kit Rachlis and John Ferguson at the *Boston Phoenix*, Richard Goldstein at the *Village Voice*, and Katherine Koberg at the *Seattle Weekly*, all of whom steered me gently away from ponderous academese and helped me to narrow the gap between good criticism and good scholarly writing. To them, and to my family and friends in England who extended long-distance support, I am grateful beyond words.

1

Introduction
Cultural Analysis and Social Change

This book grew out of an interest in television entertainment during one of the liveliest periods in its history, the 1970s, when major shifts in network policy, responding to broader cultural changes, helped produce some of the medium's most innovative programming. I was interested in the dialogue between television imagery and other kinds of interpretation of the cultural life of the 1970s in the United States. My particular concern was with the light that changing themes in television could shed on certain issues that were preoccupying cultural critics and social scientists during this period: the tendency to describe America as a culture in crisis and to fasten on family life as the troubled center of that crisis; the relationship between family and work; and more broadly changing perceptions of the boundaries between public and private spheres of everyday life.

My aim was to explore the changing social psychology of family life with respect to changing definitions of "normal families" in a fictional medium whose imagery has always been fundamentally familial. The ubiquity of television and its intensely domestic character make it an ideal narrative form in which to observe changing ideas about family. It is watched by a vast number of people in their homes; its advertising is geared to both the parts and the whole of the family unit; its images, in both news and entertainment, are stamped with the familial. Even its workplace settings are shot through with domesticity. Given the sheer breadth of its appeal, television tends to address—and help create—widely held beliefs that permeate the culture rather than the minority views at its margins.

I began my investigations with a quite orthodox Parsonian reading of the meanings of *family* and *workplace*. A family was to be understood as a network of social relations marking out the private sphere—that is, a group of people tied by blood or marriage; living under the same roof; organized by a hierarchy of authority, mutual obligation, and privilege; assuming the defined roles and statuses associated with "traditional" extended and "modern" nuclear families; and providing its members with primary supports and constraints cemented by emotional as well as economic interdependence. By contrast, a workplace embodied the secondary aspects of social life—specific occupational goals; segmented social relationships with limited emotional content; the principal site of participation in the public sphere.

As my work progressed, it became clear that more flexible definitions of the key terms were required for both television and the "real world." In the language of prime-time television in the 1970s, both family and workplace became implicated in a broader meditation on primary affiliation, an imaginative commentary on community and collective solidarity grounded in the disruptive changes of modern life in the late twentieth century. The recurring imagery of television's dominant genre, the episodic series, conferred on both family and workplace the intimacy and emotional intensity of family, albeit in significantly different ways. Chapter 4 demonstrates how in shows with explicit family settings, such as *All in the Family* and *One Day at a Time*, the home became a repository for conflict, anxiety, and fear about the fracturing of family life and the corrosive effects of social change; the haven was transformed into a place of siege. The television workplace described in Chapter 5, by contrast, assumed the warmth and solidarity, the emotional intensity and nourishment, and the protective functions of the families and communities we believe we once had, and have lost.

Taken together, the television family and workplace served to map out a social field, recasting the boundaries between private and public spheres and redefining the normative meanings within and between those spheres. The television workplaces of *The Mary Tyler Moore Show*, *M*A*S*H*, and *Lou Grant* came to provide a more plausible terrain than the home for public and private to intersect, a haven within the simultaneously heartless and intrusive world of the corporate organization. The emergence of an ethic of "professionalism" in television occupations, defined as a "people's advocacy" resting on commitment, cooperation, and substantive rather than formal skills, served both as a critique of corporate power and an alternative vision of desirable public leadership.

This portrayal of family and work and the relations between them differs sharply from that depicted on television in either the two preceding decades or in the 1980s. As Chapter 2 shows, the families and workplaces of prime-time television in the 1950s and 1960s served as the harmonious, well-oiled building blocks of a benignly conceived American society founded in affluence and consensus. In Chapter 6 I argue that in the 1980s television has generated a variety of family forms, presided over by the intact nuclear families of *The Cosby Show, Family Ties,* and other shows.

These shifts raise interesting questions about the relationship of television to prevailing social concerns in different periods. Television is no more a mirror to (or an escape from) the social world than any other fictional narrative. True, television's naturalism feeds our expectations of verisimilitude. Its mimetic visual form persuades us that Ozzie Nelson (of *Ozzie and Harriet*) lives on, schmoozing the day away with his neighbor across the yard; that the Bunkers (of *All in the Family*) really live in Queens; and that the Huxtables (of *The Cosby Show*) frolic day after day in a well-appointed Manhattan town house. But family life never resembled that of the Nelsons, the Bunkers, or the Huxtables, at least not in any narrow sociological sense. Like all storytelling, television speaks to our collective worries and to our yearning to improve, redeem, or repair our individual or collective lives, to complete what is incomplete, as well as to our desire to know what is going on out there in that elusive "reality." Television comments upon and orders, rather than reflects, experience, highlighting public concerns and cultural shifts.

The disjuncture between real and television families and the shifts in both also caution us to proceed with care when we interpret short-term cultural changes, especially in American television, which is by nature faddish. The sheer volume of its ephemeral output; the fierce competition between the networks; their common fear of the commercial threat from cable and pay television, and of the power of home video and other new technologies to restructure viewing habits—all these constraints press into the routines of programming a demand for constant novelty with relatively little innovation. Even the most successful series usually lasts no longer than seven years, which, some critics argue, suggests that changes in genre or style have little significance as indices of social trends. Fads, however, are more than whims; Chapter 3 suggests that fads with staying power can tell us much about the ways people respond to social change. As advertisers and broadcasters try to second-guess the public mood (a daunting project, even if such a unitary zeitgeist existed), they pay earnest attention to what they consider to be the mirrors of public concern, namely, the media themselves. Television feeds off itself and other media, and in this way its images both echo and participate in the shaping of cultural trends. Buzzwords like *the sixties, the me-decade*, and *yuppies* are casually threaded through the rhetoric of television, become enshrined in programming knowledge and routines, and pass into the currency of everyday social exchange. That makes them important, however short-lived.

Short-term changes, too, may be seen as the redefinition of older concerns. Television, after all, is little more than forty years old, but it inherits the forms and preoccupations of earlier narratives and social meanings. If the television narrative is playing in new ways with commonly understood boundaries between private and public spheres, we should not assume that confusion about boundaries is new. The longer historical view reminds us that cultural forms are always in dialogue with the disruptions that social change inflicts on everyday life. If the felt shock of the new can be traced in any era, the specific caste of this concern and its framing in social thought have changed with time and place. "Histories of the arts," observed Frank Kermode in a 1986 essay, "are histories of past modernities."

The interplay of short- and long-term cultural analysis, then, suggests that television's juggling of the meanings of private and public, family and work, rehearses older questions in a new social environment. The troubled distinction between the "inner" and "outer" lives of individuals and groups has formed the backbone of nineteenth-century classical social thought and has proved seminal to the modernist sensibility of Western politics and culture since the turn of the century.[1] In the eyes of many social historians, the scale and speed of change precipitated by industrial and bureau-cratic divisions of labor threatened to fragment the individual and collective frameworks that ordered everyday life. Intellectual debate about the character of social change has tended to indulge in the broadest of conceptual and historical polarities: traditional and modern, modern and postmodern, capitalist and postcapitalist. Short-term cultural analysis can enrich the debate by lending it specificity, documenting particular themes that deepen and qualify conceptual sweeps of continuity and change. The 1970s (loosely defined as the period between 1968 and 1980) are of particular interest to cultural historians because the period is marked by an unusually intense propensity for self-scrutiny, reflected in an acceleration of the trend begun in the 1950s and 1960s for diagnostic cultural analyses offering varieties of zeitgeist for modernity. By 1968 many of these had begun to betray a pervasive anxiety, pessimism, and foreboding about the collapse of community and the growing fragmentation of social life.

This grim mood was captured in the titles and prefatory quotations of several prominent works that spanned the decade. Philip Rieff's *The Triumph of the Therapeutic* (1968), an account of the replacement of religious faith with a privatized, psychologistic world view, began with a long excerpt from Yeats's poem *The Second Coming,* whose famous line "things fall apart, the centre cannot hold" has since graced the flyleaf of several volumes of cultural criticism. Philip Slater's *The Pursuit of Loneliness* (1970) was subtitled *American Culture at the Breaking Point.* Historian Christopher Lasch's two major works of cultural analysis, *Haven in a Heartless World* (1977) and *The Culture of Narcissism: American Life in an Age of Diminishing Expectations* (1979), similarly intimated a sense of crisis and social disintegration in the transition from "economic" to "therapeutic" modes of social control and aspiration.

Particularly striking in the frequency and intensity of its appearance in public and intellectual discourse was the debate about the contemporary nuclear family and the growing perception of family life as, if not the source, then certainly the central arena for the expression of social conflict. Again and again the literature pointed to family trouble as the center of modern malaise. Substantive changes in patterns of marriage and family life during this period, such as the rise in rates of divorce and remarriage, single-parent families, dual-career families, and singles living alone suggested swift and radical changes in family structure.[2] The growing literature in research and policy on family pathology and family violence, stimulated in part by official fears concerning the growing dependence of families on welfare agencies, in part by the focus on the family as the unit of care in therapeutic institutions, was more often than not appropriated as signaling the impending collapse of family life.

Renewed interest in the sociology and history of consciousness in the 1970s, a legacy of the cultural radicalism of the 1960s, set the stage for a wave of ethnographic studies as well as more speculative essays in the sociology of culture that tried to dig beneath statistical and demographic data to examine the social psychology of family life. Among the more controversial of the latter was Christopher Lasch's *Haven in a Heartless World*. Lasch's argument built on the Frankfurt School critique, which identified the roots of current family decay in capitalist development itself. The separation of production and consumption into work and leisure in the early capitalist period was, he argued, later consolidated by the socialization of both production and reproduction. Thus a split between private and public life was introduced, according to Lasch, only to have the boundaries blurred by the intrusion of state and corporate authority. The rationalized workplace, organized by principles of scientific management, was being echoed in the domestic sphere, in the expropriation of family skills, autonomy, and authority by professional experts of the modern therapeutic state. In Lasch's view, the loss of the paternal authority so deeply entrenched in the classical bourgeois family of early capitalism eliminated the oedipal struggle between generations, which he regarded as indispensable to moral growth. The disastrous consequences he forecast for individual development and collective life were elaborated in his later books *The Culture of Narcissism* and *The Minimal Self*.

One response to the deepening sense of trouble in the family was the beginning of a call from the right for a "return to traditional values." As one prominent feminist critic noted:

If there is one cultural trend that has defined the seventies, it is the aggressive resurgence of family chauvinism, flanked by its close relatives, antifeminism and homophobia. The right's impassioned defense of traditional family values . . . has affected the social atmosphere even in the liberal, educated middle class that produced the cultural radicals. The new consensus is that the family is now our last refuge, our only defense against universal predatory selfishness, loneliness, and rootlessness; the idea that there could be desirable alternatives to the family is no longer taken seriously.

(Willis 1982, 150)

Other observers of contemporary domestic life took a more sanguine view of these changes. Proponents of the "new social history" sought to unmask the nostalgic myth of a solidary preindustrial extended family, emphasizing the deepening emotional coherence of modern family relationships (Shorter 1975). Mary Jo Bane's (1976) review of sociological data on the family led her to stress both the continuity and adaptive capacity of the nuclear family and conclude that the family was not disintegrating but evolving in the direction of a healthy pluralism. In the wave of family ethnographies that sprang up during this period, there was little evidence to support Bane's optimism. Most painted a far from rosy picture, pointing especially to the misery, conflict, and insecurity of working-class families under severe economic and psychic pressure.[3] At best, "cultures of resistance" were observed in strong networks of solidarity and support among women (Stack 1974).

Although there were few ethnographic studies of middle class family life in the 1970s, statistical data showed that divorce rates and other indices of family pathology, while apparently higher among low-income families, were substantial and rising in upper socioeconomic groups too. Historical context and the changing priorities of research and policy interests suggest caution in inferring significant social change from statistical shifts alone. What seems clear, however, is that during this period social problems were being framed in the public mind as family problems, not only by official agencies and social scientists, but also in the imagery of popular culture. Chapter 4 shows how, in the new domestic comedies of prime-time television, the family leaped into the foreground as a veritable circus of conflict and change. This should not be read as a rejection of family since alongside the overwhelming anxiety about family and marriage there streamed a persistent yearning for the close ties of family and community and a subtext exploring new forms and new rules for family living.

Similar concerns were surfacing in other pop-culture forms. One of the most successful films to close the 1960s was *The Graduate*, which dealt with the counterculture and generational conflict within the frame of suburban family ennui. And the 1970s drew to a close with a wave of films like *Ordinary People* and *Kramer versus Kramer* that expressed the pain of family collapse underpinned by a longing for new ways of domestic living. The popularity of psychotherapeutic self-help manuals on best-seller lists testified to the concern with emotional relationships that Bane extolled, but it did not in itself imply increasing emotional coherence. If anything, it bore witness to a mounting sense of intractable trouble at home and a preoccupation with individual fulfillment at the expense of commitment to marriage and family. "Who can easily imagine a young son or daughter marrying or living with the same person for close to fifty years? Or with two for twenty-five years each?" wrote Elizabeth Hardwick (1978, 9) in a special issue of *Daedalus* devoted to "a new America." Indeed, throughout the 1970s "youth" became a prominent metaphor for the social divisions of the time, defined as a "generation gap" and framed within the family. One popular interpreter of cultural trends went so far as to assert that "by way of a dialectic Marx could never have imagined, technocratic America produces a potentially revolutionary element among its own youth. The bourgeoisie, instead of discovering the class enemy in its factories, finds it across the breakfast table in the person of its own pampered children" (Roszak 1969, 34). Some of the most popular television shows drew on that image, not least because, as Chapter 3 demonstrates, television programmers were beginning to pay close attention to the new generation of college-educated young people who were likely both to wield the large disposable incomes that advertisers sought to attract, and to become the cultural opinion leaders of the future.

The other demographic group that had always interested programmers and advertisers was, of course, women, who did the bulk of family buying and who watched a good deal of television. It was thus inevitable that the issues raised by the women's movement, arguably the most vigorous and broadly based survivor of the radical movements of the 1960s, would find their way into television, in the form of a "prime-time feminism" described in Chapters 4 and 5. Alongside the felt concern about increasing pressures on domestic life, feminists sought to foster a more critical spirit toward traditional family arrangements and gender divisions and a greater openness to new, less patriarchal family forms. Some called for a reexamination of the assumptions underpinning debate about the family. Taking issue with Lasch and the "new family history" as well as the cheerful family pluralism espoused by Bane, they argued that interpretation of family pathology and conflict as well as broader speculation about the quality of family life must be grounded in an understanding of the politics of public concern about the family.

Some feminists agreed with Lasch that the separation of work and home and the imposition of capitalist work-discipline created severe stresses in family life while at the same time advancing the rhetoric of family solidarity; but they reminded those who, with Lasch, mourned the erosion of patriarchal authority that family stability (as measured by the absence of divorce or separation) was not synonymous with family health or happiness. Indeed, they argued, the patriarchal family achieved its apparent calm at the high cost of the repression of women and children. Moreover, the limited gains of more flexible, democratic family forms had merely opened a space for feminism that must be fought for constantly. In their view, the modern family continued to reproduce inequalities, not only of gender, but also of class and race.[4]

If the feminist critique offered a useful warning against romanticizing both the precapitalist and the nuclear families, it also, through its concern with stresses in the lives of working women, slowly but persistently drew attention to the links between family and workplace—a largely neglected area of research despite the growing number of government-sponsored and social-scientific studies on work and quality of life. The years following World War II had established the large corporation as the typical employer for most working adults. By the late 1960s most workers were salaried employees in rationalized, bureaucratic organizations. It was clear by this time that postwar optimism about the prospects for unlimited economic growth and affluence could not be sustained. Prompted in part by the fluctuating fortunes of the American economy, in part by the coming of age of a generation concerned with building cooperative relationships for a meaningful life at home and at work, government and academic research began to focus on worker dissatisfaction and other sources of workplace strain—qualitative aspects of the work experience that transcended narrower criteria of productivity and efficiency.[5]

By the early 1970s the growing presence in the labor force of women and young "baby boomers" with substantial career aspirations began to raise questions of meaning in the workplace and to motivate a reassessment of older concerns about the relationship of career to family life. The concerns and outlooks of these two groups, whose prominence in the countercultural movements of the 1960s and strong representation in the workplace were helping to redefine the meaning of work, were of more than passing interest to programming executives seeking to attract affluent and influential viewers within the "mass" audience. Surveying the literature on work and family, Kanter (1977b) noted that whereas official reports tended to regard *unemployed* men as "social problems" during this period, it was *employed* women who were thus defined both in official reports and in social-scientific studies since their presence in the workplace was perceived as a threat to their responsibilities as wives and mothers. Feminist critics and activists reformulated the problem, insisting on the right of women to work and to receive the same pay as male workers while pointing to the particular difficulties faced by women, the majority of whom were working mothers in low-paying routine jobs. With the divorce rate and the number of unmarried mothers (especially teenage mothers) rising, a growing proportion were also single parents, but married women too continued for the most part to shoulder the burdens of childrearing and homemaking. Those whose partners were willing to share these tasks had to negotiate with employers who typically were far from amenable to rearranging work schedules around shared parenting. The struggle over corporate provision for working mothers through child care, flexible schedules, and other strategies continued in the 1980s.

The mass entry of women into the workplace, together with the cultural movements of the 1960s, also encouraged a shift of emphasis from individual performance and achievement to cooperation and caretaking in the workplace. As recent studies have shown, however, employers can turn the caring orientation women have brought to the workplace to their own advantage. Kanter's (1977a) research on corporate women, wives, and secretaries suggests that the "feminization" of the workplace also serves to lock women into subordinate and exploited roles to the extent that they reproduce their traditional family roles at work.[6] Chapter 5 describes the obsessive rehearsal of this problem in television shows featuring career women.

Given these changes, the relative absence in the research literature of a sustained discussion of the connections between conflict in the family and in the workplace is remarkable. In social-scientific thought, Kanter observed, the "myth of separate worlds" was sustained by the dominance of the Parsonian distinction between work as the arena of universalistic, specific, emotionally neutral, and performance-oriented norms, and family as the preserve of particularistic, diffuse, emotional, and ascribed norms. Historically, the perceived split between work and home, between public and private domains, was established in the early period of industrial organization. But it was always a problematic division, and as corporate organization began to reach deeper into areas hitherto reserved as "private" in the twentieth century, the boundaries between work and leisure became blurred.[7] Kanter's research has shown how family life has taken on more rationalized ("home economics") and scientific ("domestic science") elements as its dependence on state and corporate supervision has grown. Similarly, organizations have tended to develop internal cultures with decidedly ascriptive and affective characteristics.

Confusion about the division between public and private spheres, and a yearning for community in public as well as private life, have thus long been articulated as concerns in public discourse. The tendency of professions to build internal cultures—"collective representations" of the world—and of professionals to seek community through work dates back at least to the late nineteenth century. In *The Division of Labor* Durkheim looked to occupational groups to provide a basis for moral community in modern societies with complex divisions of labor. And in Progressive-era America the attempt to reconcile principles of bureaucratic rationalism and scientific management with ideals of public service and community was a persistent theme among the new middle class. Studies of specific occupational milieux, as well as of broad occupational categories differentiated by social class, suggest a distinction between more and less "absorptive" occupations, between employees for whom work culture is more central and those who must frame the meaning of work in more instrumental terms.[8] Work and family, concluded Kanter in a synthetic analysis of these studies, are probably least separate for people in "involving high human contact jobs"—notably professional, human service, intellectual, and upper-executive positions—"whose families want to be up-to-date and thus adopt values from recent social consensus" (Kanter 1977b, 77). These are precisely the demographic groups network programmers sought to attract to their shows in the 1970s.

In the United States, where work has traditionally taken precedence over private life, it is also likely that organizations intrude more into family life than the other way around, especially in absorptive occupations. Stable families may produce more reliable workers, but insofar as the family offers a competing source of loyalty and authority, it poses a threat to rational bureaucracy and organizational commitment. Faced with the dilemma of whether to co-opt, exclude, or replace domestic ties, organizations have historically shown ambivalence toward families, moving between all three strategies.

Corporations have always, to greater or lesser degrees, colonized the rhetoric and rituals of family in order to foster employee loyalty. In the early 1970s, with American industry entering a period of economic instability and retrenchment, and with the size and scale of corporate life growing ever larger, the question of organizational commitment became critical. Many industries renewed their efforts to promote family-style allegiances through the creation of "corporate cultures," an organizational buzzword during this period. To judge by the tenor of social and cultural thought on work in corporate America, this "familialization" was to be interpreted less as an index of growing cohesiveness in organizations than as a measure to shore up, not merely productivity and efficiency, but also the flagging morale and loyalty of a work force increasingly ambivalent toward organizations whose success they had once equated with their own advancement. The problem was aggravated by the entry into the labor force of an unusually large cohort of college graduates. Some, influenced by the movements of the 1960s, were critical of corporate enterprise in general. Others with substantial career ambitions could quickly become disillusioned with the gap between their qualifications and the attenuated options open to them. When Paul Leinberger interviewed some of

William II. Whyte's original "organization men" in 1986, he found among them a pervasive sense of disappointment and betrayal, whereas their children, now executives themselves, exhibited a far more segmented and contingent commitment to their employers than had their parents. Michael Maccoby's (1976) study of corporate executives portrayed a new breed of organization men, whose flimsy attachment to the corporation hinged on its capacity to sustain their self-images as "winners." Chapter 5 illustrates the variety of forms in which this crisis of commitment is clothed in the television workplaces of the 1970s.

The image of a work ethic severed from its transcendent ties to moral and social progress finds strong echoes in other pop-culture forms. Elizabeth Long's (1985) analysis of themes of success in best-selling novels in postwar America traces the gradual slide of the work ethic that lay at the heart of the American Dream into crisis and disarray. The equation of individual progress with public progress in the benignly conceived social order of the early 1950s gave way by the early 1960s to a retreat, in the face of corporate demands on personal life, to the suburban family as that haven in a heartless world whose passing Lasch was to lament a decade later. By the mid-1970s best-sellers pictured a world in full-blown crisis, with families and organizations fragmented and lacking in meaning or purpose. Long's reading of 1970s novels sketches a Goffmanian world of impression managers for whom success became a matter of personal style, of having and being rather than doing, and a cynical conformity contingent on rapid personal advancement.

Best-selling novels tend to articulate the sensibilities of their predominantly middle-class readership. Television, because of the wider sweep of its social orbit, has always been more resolutely populist. In the early 1970s, though, the industry began to carve out a constituency of middle-class viewers within its more traditional mass audience. The sheer increase in the number of television shows (especially comedies) with workplace settings by the mid-1970s may have reflected a conscious effort to appeal to this new target audience of career-oriented upscale viewers presumed to favor work over family goals. The television workplace addressed itself, too, to the crisis of authority and organizational commitment. The creation of a protective, peer-oriented enclave within an organization portrayed as filled with scheming, callous, or stupid but powerful functionaries offered a critique of corporate and professional life that may have spoken to the disappointment experienced by many hopeful careerists at the blocking of their progress by a stagnant economy.

There was, however, a more powerful appeal in the television workplace, which began to offer itself as a caring alternative to the home, a displacement of the yearning for a fulfilling family life onto the workplace. Hence the centrality of women in shows like *The Mary Tyler Moore Show* or "woman-like" nurturant father figures in *Barney Miller* and *Taxi*, who defined the meaning of work in terms of caring relationships rather than individualized achievement. It was no accident that the typical television workplace was not a gleaming corridor of power but a decrepit (if cozy) and barely functioning corner of the organizational world, in which human worth was measured by loyalty and humanistic values rather than contracts negotiated or projects completed. Indeed, for wider audiences, the warm involvement of the television workplace may have provided compensation for the dull, dehumanized workplaces so many of them faced in their everyday lives. And if the setting up of corporate functionaries, psychiatrists, and lawyers as the new television villains expressed the same fear and resentment found in cultural criticism toward the growing power of a large "new class" of managerial and professional experts, it also created a symbolic mastery of that fear.[9] Redefining the ethics of professionalism in populist terms may have subtly reassured viewers who regarded the intellectual qualifications of professionals with suspicion or skepticism that *some* professionals were on their side. Durkheim might have been entertained (more likely horrified) by the idea that his hopes for an ethical oasis within an immoral or amoral institutional world would be realized on television.

The television work-family, then, expressed a cultural dilemma: on the one hand, the yearning for meaning and community in the workplace, and on the other, the fear of the power of corporations and of professionals in corporate settings. In the imagery of television, as in much intellectual commentary at the time, this fear deepened into a vague but pervasive post-Watergate mistrust by ordinary Americans of the political and economic institutions that shaped their lives from a great distance and of the elites who dominated the corporate sector.

Diagnosing the age, cultural critics viewed the 1970s as a decade of retreat into grim survival, in contrast to the more elevated mood of the 1960s, which were often characterized as a period of limitless horizons in collective efforts for social change. Some pointed to a turning inward, a retreat into the self and a fascination with psychotherapies of various kinds in the pursuit of personal fulfillment. Social critics of the left and right deplored the spread of an individualism stripped of wider social obligation. There were those who linked the preoccupation with self more generally to the deracinating qualities of modern culture and the deterioration of communal frameworks that once embedded the individual in public life.[10]

If the prevailing tone of cultural criticism was pessimistic, it was not exclusively so. Some identified pockets of local collective organization as encouraging signs of resistance to the centralized power of corporate America (Lasch 1979). Alongside the anomie Long (1985) found in the best-selling novels of the decade, she detected a growing openness and heterogeneity, a pluralism that signaled a new flexibility in the American popular imagination, and a relativism that foreshadowed the celebration of the freedoms brought by the modern experience found in some cultural criticism in the 1980s (Berman 1982), even as it sparked a sense of foreboding in others (Bellah et al. 1985). Feminists pointed out that the erosion of the traditional family structure might be a necessary stage in the struggle for the freedom and equality of women.

In general, though, the literature in social science and cultural criticism in the 1970s points to a mounting confusion about the rules and frameworks ordering daily life in modern America, in particular the location of conflict and distress within the family and at the intersection of family and work, private and public spheres. The narratives of television, as will be seen in Chapters 4 and 5, worked on these concerns and resolved them in their own particular ways.

Taking the decade as a unit of interpretive analysis is a tricky enterprise, not least because it runs the risk of forcing the historical issues. The focus on short-term developments creates the possibility of converting continuity into change, elevating minor developments to the status of major shifts, and missing the seeds of genuine cultural change. In a 1980 Boston lecture Susan Sontag described the urge to frame social change in decades as a peculiarly modern habit, replacing the nineteenth-century emphasis on the century as well as the more recent preoccupation with generation and reflecting a growing tendency to miniaturize time, albeit in dazzlingly macroscopic ways. To periodize an era, she argued, confers on it a mythic ideological load, attributing to it particular moods, hierarchies of significance, and conditions. In a visual culture that increasingly replaces substance with image, people like the decade because the quantification implied in the naming lends weight and objectivity to language, making life appear more real, less bewildering, and more easily controlled.

To this might be added the argument that the attribution of a particular style or mood (the "me-decade," the "culture of narcissism") implies a unitary cultural consensus, a zeitgeist that does violence to the modern experience, which is precisely fragmented and splintered, not just by the loosening bonds of communal life, but also by the sharp divisions of class, race, gender, and age. For Sontag, "decade thinking" is culturally and politically negative since it invites the packaging and containing of experience and damages the capacity to pay attention to time in different and more active ways. For the sociologist of culture, however, the decade justifies itself precisely because it is a social construct, a limited range of ways of looking at the world, whose (often unintended) consequences return to shape social life. The disjunctions between everyday experience and decade style, as defined by popular culture, are only partial. Ideas with some staying power do not spring from nowhere, and if naming a decade helps to shape it, it must also have appropriated elements within the culture. Casual and reductive as the term *me-decade* may be, it refers to the sense of social isolation and disembodied individualism that pervades many forms of cultural expression in the 1970s. Indeed, the naming of a decade (that felt sense of the quality of life termed by Raymond Williams in his earlier work the "structure of feelings"), in which mass-mediated meanings play such a central role, is a pivotal concern of this project. The whirl of cultural fashions that television promotes may be an integral part of the modern structure of feelings. By exploring the range of commonly understood meanings of family and workplace in one area of mass-mediated popular culture, television entertainment, we can add to the findings of ethnographies and other qualitative sources and deepen the debate about cultural change in the 1970s.

2

Television as Family
The Episodic Series, 1946–1969

Few contemporary forms of storytelling offer territory as fertile as American television for uncovering widely received ideas about family. First, the medium's accessibility and the size and heterogeneity of its audiences make it the most truly popular (and populist) of modern cultural forms. Second, the language and imagery of family break obsessively through the surface forms of all its genres—comedy and dramatic series, daytime and nighttime soaps, made-for-TV movies, even news programming. Of all these it is the episodic series (which includes both the half-hour situation comedy and the one-hour action-adventure series) that fosters a gradual buildup of viewer attachment to individual characters and their relationships, generating the fullest possibilities for a meditation on domestic themes. In the first two decades of television entertainment the episodic series established itself as television's characteristic genre, evolving from the more traditional plotted narrative of the radio series into a continuous chronicle of domesticity that has provided a changing commentary on family life—by turns reflective, utopian, dystopian, its mood now euphoric, now anxious, now redemptive.

I am using the term *genre* here not as a fixed "essence" of a type of narrative but as the routinization of particular ways of doing things that harden into knowledge about program types recognizable to both producers and viewers as "sitcoms" or "action series." Genres are neither fixed nor immutable entities; they evolve into traditions that become modified over time. They are socially constituted and articulated discourses, or more precisely *selections* from ranges of discourse; their meanings cannot be fully understood outside the social contexts—commercial, organizational, political, cultural—in which they are made and received. Genre, accordingly, should not be read statically as a textual form with immanent structural properties but as the outcome (provisional and always subject to change) of social practices—received procedures that become objectified in the stories television tells and modified in the interpretive act of viewing. As with form, so with meaning; television's articulation of social attitudes, its shifting pictures of the recognizable frames of family and work, are filtered through the changing world views, daily priorities, and routines of producers, network executives, and advertisers, then filtered again through the varied perceptions of viewers.

Thus genre is here considered as a link between producers and audiences, a constellation of provisionally agreed codes. Genre analysis allows us to posit those conventions in the construction of television meanings that are shared by producers and viewers, without assuming a necessary symmetry between the interpretive readings of these two groups, or indeed those of critics, in specific instances. If, as Feuer (1987) argues, genre also functions as the regulation of difference, it may be seen as shaping textual meaning and disciplining the interpretive activity of creators and audiences. However varied their specific interpretations, viewers respond within the boundaries imposed by genre conventions. They know their way around the structures and rules of the sitcom and the action-adventure series; viewer response is bounded by canned laughter, studio warmups, commercial breaks, musical and visual cues, character and plot types, and of course the knowledge that accrues from the viewer's involvement with television over time. Indeed, it is likely that the implicit rules of television genres are more clearly understood by viewers than are those of the genres of other aesthetic forms by their publics. Audiences for television are more likely to know that they are watching a situation comedy than most readers are to recognize a realist novel, or moviegoers are to identify an example of *film noir*.

The domesticity that from the beginning was bred into the forms and structures of the episodic series was shaped by the industrial, technical, and aesthetic traditions that television inherited from earlier media. With its small screen, talking-heads format, and interior settings, television combines the looming proximity of film with the constraining space of the theater. It lends itself to the intimacy of character and relationship rather than to action, to the routinized intimacy of domestic life rather than to the melodramatic, eventful intensity of live theater or film. Going to the movies or to a show remains an outing, a ritualized public activity that feels special. Television sits in the home, both part of the furniture and part of the family; in many homes the television set remains on for most of the day, whether people are actively watching or not. In its own glamorous way, television celebrates the ordinary; and by doing so it suggests that certain versions of family life are normal and others deviant, strange, or (by exclusion) nonexistent.

In television, genre is an explicit industrial category organized in the service of efficiency and rationalization of a commercial product.[1] The growth of the medium into a centralized, one-way system of transmission serves the commercial interests of its corporate owners and backers more than it does any inherent technical logic. The roots of television in private enterprise and its rapid development into an industry dominated by giant corporations and advertising sponsors have been extensively documented by media historians.[2] Television's "family-style" form—its strategic location in the home and its economic dependence on advertising aimed at consumer families—was shaped by an industrial structure inherited directly from radio, whose resources and distribution were concentrated in the hands of the major networks, CBS and NBC in the 1920s, with ABC joining them in the 1930s.

After World War II, which called a temporary halt to technological advances in "radio with pictures," the same networks quickly established their sovereignty over the mass production and diffusion of television. As with other major consumer industries, corporate power was consolidated in two ways. First, the concentration of capital, despite successive attempts at antitrust legislation by the Federal Communications Commission, proceeded through integration (takeovers and mergers) of media products and organizations, diversification into other commercial areas by means of interlocking directorates, and expansion into overseas markets (Murdock and Golding 1977). Second, the power of commercial broadcasters was cemented from the beginning by a strategic alliance with advertising sponsors (Barnouw 1978). During the 1950s major corporations like U.S. Steel, Goodyear, Kraft, and

Philco literally owned whole shows, which gave them substantial control over production and, by extension, over content. Indeed, until the end of the decade each studio housed a "sponsor's booth," from which company officials supervised the dress rehearsals of live television shows, often insisting on last-minute changes in material they considered threatening to their marketing goals or too controversial for the "average viewer."

By the mid-1950s, with cinema attendance falling steadily and radio planners cannily adapting to the competition by regrouping as networks of local stations transmitting news and music, network television had become the uncrowned queen of popular entertainment. In 1950, 4.4 million families owned television sets; by 1960, 50 million sets had been sold. In a period of soaring productivity, low unemployment, and relative wealth, television became the quintessential badge of consumerism, a symbol of middle-class status and affluence in the home. Television advertising, whose primary target was families of all social classes and ethnic groups, helped establish the nuclear family in corporate eyes as the basic unit of consumption. Unlike movies, which remained a public form of mass entertainment, both radio and television invaded the home. For advertisers, whose collaboration with broadcasters was to play a formative role in the industry's development, this was a marketing bonanza. Television became a home appliance that could be used to sell other home appliances to its owners; and as time went on, it also sold, through the episodic series, an image of desirable family life with consumption casually woven into the fabric of its stories.

By the early 1960s the fundamental contours of the television industry were established. An FCC investigation of systematic rigging by sponsors of quiz show contestants curbed the power of advertisers to intervene openly in television production by forcing them to buy time slots rather than whole shows. (Nevertheless, sponsors remain a significant force in television programming. Virtually all shows, whether news, sports, or entertainment, conform to the format of short segments wrapped around commercials, and it has become an industry cliché that programs exist to deliver audiences to sponsors.) Immediate control over production was retained by the networks, who, as buyers and sellers of the major films and series, exerted much of the significant executive power within the industry, as they do today. Only news and sports programming, and occasionally variety specials, were produced by the networks themselves. After the industry moved its entertainment divisions from New York to Hollywood in the mid-1950s, prime-time programming became the province of outside producers: the Hollywood studios, which were initially hostile to television but rapidly adapted with the sharp decline in movie attendance in the years after the War, and independent production companies, who sold their shows to the networks for syndication (Barnouw 1975).

Until its modes of production were routinized, however, television entertainment was lifted wholesale from radio. The episodic series took shape only slowly alongside the other radio entertainment formulas television was plundering—the variety shows, game shows, and "anthology series," which also mimicked the aesthetic forms of the theater. The classic variety shows, like Milton Berle's *Texaco Star Theater* and Sid Caesar's *Your Show of Shows,* grew out of radio comedy, which had based itself on turn-of-the-century vaudeville. The comedy-variety format flourished briefly but was soon eclipsed by the more predictable episodic series, and today television variety is mostly confined to occasional "specials."

In the second half of the 1950s prime-time schedules were studded with game shows like *The Price Is Right* and Groucho Marx's *You Bet Your Life,* many of which had started out as radio quiz shows. They were cheap and easy to produce, and the prizes provided the clearest form of advertising. Some, like *Strike It Rich* and *Queen for a Day,* combined quiz-type questions with hard-luck stories from contestants specially chosen for the tragic or bizarre problems that plagued their lives. The most devastating cases won the biggest prizes by audience vote, a system that implied that the balm, if not the solution, for everyday suffering was further consumption. But in 1959 the "quiz show scandals" dealt a crippling blow to prime-time game shows, and by the early 1960s many had disappeared or had been relegated to daytime schedules, where the popularity of game shows remains undiminished.

The so-called anthologies were essentially live theater plays filmed for television audiences, often exploring the growing urban problems—poverty, racism, and class and ethnic conflict—that lay just beneath the surface of postwar optimism. Major corporations sponsored whole series of individual dramas, some of which, like Paddy Chayefsky's *Marty*, Arthur Penn's *The Miracle Worker*, and Rod Serling's *Requiem for a Heavyweight*, became classics and earned for this period its reputation as the "golden age of television." In television's earliest years in New York the anthologies represented an attempt to establish artistic credentials by making television as much like the theater as possible while addressing the concerns of the large, heterogeneous audiences of postwar urban America.

Despite the critical acclaim they attracted and their initial success with audiences, the live anthologies proved a short-lived genre for commercial television. There were immediate organizational and political reasons for their decline. The move from live production in New York to filmed production in Hollywood in the early 1950s took television out of the more flexible, innovative orbit of theater and into the rationalized, more single-mindedly commercial world of the movie industry. Sponsors, too, grew nervous about the preoccupation of anthologies with intractable social problems that pointed up ironic contrasts to the happy world conjured by their commercials. Sponsorship turned rapidly into censorship, and by the end of the decade, with the reliable successes of the episodic comedies and action-adventure shows at hand, the anthologies were dropped. Today the form survives in PBS (public television) series like *American Playhouse* and as a pale ghost in made-for-TV movies, which, like the anthologies, focus on contemporary social problems and wrap up a complete story in one viewing.

Political considerations aside, the formats of the anthologies, variety shows, and game shows were, from a commercial point of view, inefficient. They were not sufficiently rationalized, not *formulaic* enough for an industry in which profitability superseded all other criteria and reliable success, as measured by audience ratings, was the primary goal of programmers. The rapid turnover of variety show stars and game show contestants, the complete stories with different actors each week that the anthologies had inherited from theater and film, and—above all—the spontaneity of live television lacked the continuity and predictability that would build program loyalty and (advertisers hoped) brand name loyalty among viewers. Television had from the first been set up like radio—a home appliance for regular use. The episodic series, built on the twin principles of plot repetition and continuity of character, reflected broadcasters' efforts to find tried-and-true recipes for success that would regularly deliver a mass audience to the corporate sponsors. Genre, in this instance, developed in part as a strategy for shaping and controlling audience response.

Television is often criticized on aesthetic grounds for its formulaic character. Yet all genre conventions, whether in television, the novel, or the epic poem, are formulaic to the degree that they build on prior forms and can be understood and recognized, or "placed," in relation to other forms by their audiences. Viewers may recognize Archie Bunker not just as a sociological type—the working-class bigot—but also as the direct descendant of Ralph Kramden and Chester Riley. Modern popular culture in particular, because of the broad base of its appeal and its diffusion through the mass media, must achieve simplicity and ready comprehensibility, the bold brush strokes of plot and character that produce instant familiarity. In the United States, network television extends these principles with particular force because its industrial development has proceeded largely unchecked by noncommercial goals.[3] Television's copycat homogeneity, its endless rehearsal of the same themes, and the plundering of successful formulas within and between networks are often attributed to the cynicism of producers or to the philistinism or laziness of viewers. But copying the work of others is not, or not only, a reflection of producers' assumptions about the mediocrity of public taste. It is embedded in the routine practices of network television, in the common fund of knowledge about how television is made. The term *formula* is, like genre, used here as an industrial rather than a strictly aesthetic category. Imitation, repetition, and recombination are part and parcel of the logic of the television industry, a response to the need to achieve quick and regular profits in the face of escalating overhead and acute uncertainty about audience preferences. Quick profits are made by selling program time to advertisers at high rates, and sales in television are determined by program ratings.

Much has been written and said about the crudity of the Nielsen ratings as a measure of the relative popularity of networks and programs.[4] In the early years the ratings offered rather attenuated data, based on a small, randomly selected sample of "Nielsen families" whose television sets were equipped with "audimeters," which told broadcasters how many sets were tuned in to a particular channel in a given time period. Journals (usually completed by women in the Nielsen households) gave additional, if less reliable, information about who was watching what, and when. Even today, with the use of the more sophisticated "people meters," the Nielsen ratings fall short as qualitative measures; that is, they offer little systematic information about *how* people watch, whether they like what they see, or indeed whether they are watching at all. And given the similarity of network offerings, ratings measure viewers' choices within the rather narrow range of what they are offered.

Regardless of their validity, however, in the 1950s and 1960s the Nielsen ratings were virtually the only source of information about audience activity available to producers and network executives. They were central to network programming decisions and, in the eyes of sponsors, offered proof of program desirability as advertising space. Moreover, during this period the ratings system conceived of its audiences not as a diverse body of viewers but as an undifferentiated mass audience watching as *family units*. Just as there is no such thing as a "typical viewer," so there are no "typical families." But the creation of Nielsen families during television's first two decades expressed precisely the search for a mass audience composed of average families with predictable viewing habits. The episodic series—the family comedies and dramatic series—catered to that search by fashioning images of "normal" domestic life and serving them up to the masses they projected.

Family Comedy—The End of Ideology

By the 1958–1959 season nine out of the ten most popular shows were episodic series. Growing out of a marriage between Hollywood movie production and the established genres of network radio, the series began to evolve in two major forms, the half-hour family comedy and the one-hour drama (usually a Western or other action-adventure show). As in radio, both comedies and dramas were produced in fifteen-minute segments wrapped around advertisements. In both, too, the stars, rather than the plots, were central, and often a show would take its star's name for its title (as in *I Love Lucy* and *The Adventures of Ozzie and Harriet*), a practice that continues to underscore the pivotal significance of regular characters and the actors who play them as a focus of viewer identification. Each weekly "chapter" or episode carried a complete story or stories, written to a formula around the star's character—a format that offered viewers both the pleasure of narrative closure and the satisfaction of a continuing relationship with favorite characters. Since that steady relationship assured broadcasters of regular audiences, they too were pleased with a formula that lent itself to reruns in any order, making a show ideal for future syndication, which promised to be a lucrative source of additional revenue.

Initially shows like *Amos 'n' Andy, I Love Lucy,* and *Ozzie and Harriet* bore the stamp of radio comedy with the plot or "situation" turning on misunderstandings or absurd adventures, and the stars "talking out" their monologues or dialogues (essentially a series of running jokes) at the audience as would a stand-up comedian. But as continuity was established, viewers were invited to identify more with character than with situation, and humor hinged on the idiosyncrasies of the central characters, in particular on the relations between them. *The Burns and Allen Show* offers a perfect example of this modification. George Burns began as an omniscient narrator, inviting the viewer to join in his amused commentary on Gracie Allen's antics, which he watched on a television set within television. The stand-up routines increasingly gave way to fuller stories, with George becoming a part of the action rather than a detached observer. George's integration into the group signals the tendency that was to characterize all episodic series, whether comedy or drama, for stars to become embedded in ensembles of characters whose bonds, regardless of ties of blood or marriage, were those of family or community.[5]

A quick survey of the major sitcoms of the 1950s suggests a vast middle class of happy American families who had already made it to the choicer suburbs (*Leave It to Beaver, Ozzie and Harriet, Father Knows Best*) or were on their way there (*I Love Lucy*) or aspired to middle-class status (*The Honeymooners, The Life of Riley*). Money was a recurring theme in all these shows, whether in the relaxed assumption of affluence in *Ozzie and Harriet* or in the endless (and usually aborted) get-rich-quick schemes of Ralph Kramden and Chester Riley. If the narratives quietly extolled the virtues of

making money, they were complemented by commercials instruct-
ing viewers in how to spend it (Harriet Nelson sold Listerine and
other consumer products straight from the gleaming kitchen of her
own show)—how, in short, to become perfect consumers and, by
extension, perfect families.

As the decade wore on, television families became almost
exclusively white as well as middle-class. In a period when blacks
and rural whites were migrating north in large numbers, when race
was fast becoming a major source of urban conflict, and when
television programmers were allegedly reaching out to more
cosmopolitan audiences, the "ethnic comedies" of the early 1950s
were rapidly disappearing. *Amos 'n' Andy*, *The Goldbergs*, and *Life
with Luigi* had all been dropped from the schedules by 1954. Faced
with the promise of suburban bliss, it was assumed, *everyone* would
want a family like the Nelsons or the Cleavers. To a working class
divided by ethnic tensions and by the desire of many immigrants to
become "fully American," life with Beaver or Ricky must indeed
have seemed inviting, though it may also have generated anxieties
about not measuring up to the model they provided. Certainly
these shows have continued, in reruns, to resonate with successive
generations of younger viewers.[6] Beaver Cleaver remains a national
symbol among viewers who were not yet born during his first
incarnation, though it is likely that the particular nature of his
appeal has changed over time. Like other family comedies from the
1950s and 1960s, *Leave It to Beaver* has achieved considerable
success in reruns in the 1980s, and a cereal commercial featured
both Beaver and brother Wally as adults, evidently without
needing to announce their names. And for baby boomers who grew
up with the Beaver, an early 1980s television movie returned him
to his first fans as a true child of his generation: jobless, divorced,
and confused.

The family comedies of the 1950s articulated not so much the
realities of postwar affluence as the received wisdom of post–New
Deal capitalism: the end of ideology, a liberal-conservative dream
of a harmonious society in which the conditions for social conflict
would disappear because there would be plenty of everything to go
round. It did not matter much if Ralph Kramden's money-making
schemes collapsed; and the small mishaps of Beaver Cleaver and
Ricky Nelson played themselves out unclouded by financial

troubles, street violence, drug abuse, or marital discord. The television children of the 1950s and 1960s inhabited a universe in which mild sibling quarrels were quickly but fairly adjudicated by sage, kindly parents equipped with endless reserves of time and patience—marital teams offering clearcut rules for moral guidance. Taken together, these shows proposed family life as a charming excursion into modernity, but resting on the unshakable stability of tradition. Parents would love and respect each other and their children forever. The children would grow up, go to college, and take up lives identical in most respects to those of their parents.

If the home—and, by extension, American society—was becoming a consensual, benevolent repository for all things good, in the imagery of television evil was expelled to a recurring, fearful vision of predatory totalitarian nations. Cold-war paranoia found its way quickly into television, both in the nervous retreat from controversy stimulated by the publication of the McCarthyite *Red Channels* (a register of blacklisted media producers) in 1950 and in active anti-Soviet propaganda and generalized xenophobia. Not only comedies but also dramas and game shows were rife with anti-Communist gags and homilies (Talbot and Zheutlin 1978). Lucille Ball herself was briefly investigated for alleged Communist affiliation but was quickly "cleared" when it transpired she had registered with the Communist party for a few days in 1936 to please her grandfather (Barnouw 1975). The dichotomy of peace and justice within, and the threat of evil outside, was to be further underscored in 1960s prime-time shows about espionage (*The Untouchables, Mission Impossible*) and heroes beating back hostile aliens with totalitarian tendencies (*Star Trek*).

Comedy is a more flexible form than drama because it can create multiple, conflicting, and oppositional realities within the safe confines of the joke. Beneath the comforting middle-class conformity of 1950s sitcoms lurked tensions not so easily reconciled with prevailing norms. Lucy Ricardo's ceaseless efforts to get into show business and her rebellions against the arbitrary authority of her husband Ricky always ended in failure. Still, she never gave up; character and plot intersected repeatedly to give viewers a heroine who always bounced back to test the limits of the traditional role required of her. And when in 1960 Lucille Ball filed for divorce from Desi Arnaz, it was as if Lucy and Ricky were divorcing. But television, in the eyes of the networks, was far from ready for a divorcée as a central character, and when Lucy returned in a new series, she played a widow whose best friend was divorced. The widowed state became a popular device in 1960s comedy and drama for opening up the lives of characters to romance and increased contact with the outside world without risking the stigma of divorce. *The Brady Bunch,* one of the last of the zany "happy family" shows in this mold, brought together two widowed parents, each with three children. In the first two decades of television, widowhood may have presaged, in an acceptable way, fears about the instability of marriage and the fracturing of the nuclear family.

The anthologies too, while they lasted, provided a somber counterpoint to the bland harmony of the sitcoms. Plays like *Marty, Requiem for a Heavyweight,* and *Thunder on Sycamore Street* were rarely set among the affluent families of suburbia. Instead they rehearsed and prefigured the problems of postwar urban America—poverty, racism, alienation, family collapse—providing an insistent subtext to the visions of consensus and plenty. Insistent enough, apparently, to warrant their elimination, for by the end of the decade the withdrawal of sponsorship had virtually killed them off, and genial family comedies proliferated across the prime-time schedules of all three networks.

In 1961 the industry received an unexpected slap on the wrist from President Kennedy's newly appointed chairman of the FCC, Newton Minow. Addressing the annual meeting of the National Association of Broadcasters, he began by congratulating them on their financial success: "For your investors, the price has indeed been right." He went on, however, to tear apart the prime-time schedules, calling them a "vast wasteland" and describing them as "a procession of game shows, violence, audience participation shows, formula comedies about totally unbelievable families, blood and thunder, mayhem, violence, sadism, murder, western bad men, western good men, private eyes, gangsters, more violence, and cartoons. And endlessly, commercials—many screaming, cajoling, and offending" (Barnouw 1975, 300).

This attack, following hard on the heels of the quiz show scandals, threw the networks—briefly—into a panic. The 1961–1963 seasons brought a flurry of reforms in the shape of expanded news and public affairs programming. If Minow's speech had any long-term effects on television, it was in the growth of national and international news broadcasting and sports coverage. But with some exceptions, entertainment programming rapidly returned to the sitcoms and action-adventure shows Minow so despised. His criticisms, of course, had not struck at the heart of formula programming, television's commercial base. He had simply ordered the industry to pull up its cultural socks—which it did, fleetingly, and then returned to business as usual. Minow's "vast wasteland" speech is often cited as a watershed in television history, but it was merely symptomatic of the intermittent and largely ineffectual clucking of a regulatory agency only vaguely committed to regulation.

In general this was a period of consolidation for the television industry. The decline of single-sponsor shows and a boom in multiple sponsorship provided huge budgets for sports programming, daytime soap operas, cartoons, and a stream of light entertainment in the form of comedy-variety and action-adventure series. Overseas markets for American television were massively expanded. At home the nationalization of news bureaus and the expansion of news programs to thirty minutes increased the influence of the media on the political process. The concentration of news in the hands of the networks rather than local affiliates had the effect of filtering national and world events through the perceptions of the New York and Washington metropolitan elite as well as diminishing the local feel of earlier television news. It was in news rather than entertainment programming that the unsettled mood of the 1960s first surfaced.

For the most part the affable family comedies of the 1950s continued through much of the 1960s, in shows like *My Three Sons, Dennis the Menace, The Patty Duke Show, The Andy Griffith Show,* and *The Donna Reed Show,* all vehicles for wholesome tales set in small rural towns or comfortable middle-class suburbs of Los Angeles or New York. Once the anxiety generated by Newton Minow's speech had died down, competition between the networks to fill the prime-time schedules with new comic gimmicks escalated to fever pitch. Among the results were spooky families (*The Munsters, The Addams Family*), adult cartoons (*The Flintstones, The Jetsons*), extraterrestrials and people with magical powers (*My Favorite Martian, Bewitched, My Mother the Car*), and inept

TABLE 1. Top-Rated Prime-Time Television Programs, 1964–1965, Ranked by Audience Size (A. C. Nielsen) (October 1964–April 1965)

	Program	Network Rating		Program	Network Rating
1.	Bonanza	NBC 36.3	13.	My Three Sons	ABC 25.5
2.	Bewitched	ABC 31.0	14.	Branded	NBC 25.3
3.	Gomer Pyle, U.S.M.C.	CBS 30.7	15.	Petticoat Junction	CBS 25.2
4.	The Andy Griffith Show	CBS 28.3	16.	The Ed Sullivan Show	CBS 25.2
5.	The Fugitive	ABC 27.9	17.	Lassie	CBS 25.1
6.	The Red Skelton Show	CBS 27.4	18.	The Munsters	CBS 24.7
7.	The Dick Van Dyke Show	CBS 27.1	19.	Gilligan's Island	CBS 24.7
8.	The Lucy Show	CBS 26.6	20.	Peyton Place I	ABC 24.6
9.	Peyton Place II	ABC 26.4	21.	The Jackie Gleason Show (The Honeymooners)	CBS 24.4
10.	Combat	ABC 26.1	22.	The Virginian	NBC 24.0
11.	Walt Disney's Wonderful World of Color	NBC 25.7	23.	The Addams Family	ABC 23.9
			24.	My Favorite Martian	CBS 23.7
12.	The Beverly Hillbillies	CBS 25.6	25.	Flipper	NBC 23.4

Source. Tim Brooks and Earle Marsh. 1979. The Complete Directory to Prime Time Network TV Shows 1946–Present. New York: Ballantine Books.

Note. By the mid-1960s twenty-five of the top twenty-five shows were episodic series. Of these, thirteen were comedies and seven were dramatic series.

bumpkins (*Gilligan's Island; Gomer Pyle, U.S.M.C.*). With ratings strategies still geared toward massive, undifferentiated audiences, the rural sitcoms continued to thrive. One of the most successful was *The Beverly Hillbillies,* in which a large extended clan from the Ozarks inherited a fortune and moved to Los Angeles. The show became the last word in television populism, extolling the virtues of unpretentious rural innocence at the same time as it poked fun at the double standards, avarice, and snobbery of the Los Angeles suburban nouveaux riches.

The one series that symbolized the media-filtered sensibility of the Kennedy years was *The Dick Van Dyke Show,* a work-family comedy about a successful young television comedy writer, Rob Petrie (played by Van Dyke), and his wife, Laura (starring Mary Tyler Moore in her first major role). Much of the show's vitality came from the snappy one-liners that flew between Rob and his coworkers, Buddy and Sally (played by veteran comedians Morey Amsterdam and Rose Marie). Their cheerfully hostile banter recalled vintage radio comedy patter and anticipated the sharp verbal comedy that was to distinguish workplace comedies such as *Barney Miller* and *The Mary Tyler Moore Show* in the 1970s. The domestic scenes, though, fell squarely into the happy-family format established in the 1950s. Rob and Laura lived in connubial bliss in the up-and-coming suburb of New Rochelle, together with their son, Ritchie (Larry Matthews), who provided the cute escapades. The Petries were a young, good-looking, hard-working couple (Mary Tyler Moore was even said to look like Jackie Kennedy), modern in life-style but traditional in values. Here, too, problems presented themselves as minor misunderstandings that were always resolved within the same episode. The show advanced family life as stable and supportive, but the real spice and action went on at the office, where Rob had his own incipient work-family.

In Sally, *The Dick Van Dyke Show* had a regular female character with a challenging career, but the message was unambiguous. The show proposed separate worlds populated by two kinds of women: the world of work, which contained career girls like Sally, who was talented, funny, and a good sport even though she was mannish and plain and could not get a date; and the domestic world, which housed wives like Laura, who was pretty but unthreatening, made charming but fruitless excursions into the world of achievement,

had few creative talents, and was generally content with her role as
a supportive and eminently sensible spouse and mother. When Rob
came home, he greeted his wife with "Hi, honey, I'm home!"
whereas at work it was "C'mon, you guys!" When Laura wrote a
better children's story than her husband, she had to remind him
that "no matter what happens, you're still the best writer in the
family." By the time Laura Petrie became Mary Richards in *The
Mary Tyler Moore Show* in the 1970s, the assumptions that guided
her earlier role had been deeply compromised.

   The Dick Van Dyke Show was one of the first series to push the
domestic sitcom into the public sphere by entering the world of
work and setting up a work-family. It also transposed the 1950s
dream of middle-class prosperity and harmony into the more
sophisticated urban key of the 1960s. But the song remained the
same in all its essentials. Youth, energy, hard work, and a solid
family life still provided the ingredients for the smooth progress of
upward mobility, and anyone could harvest its rewards. Much of
the comedy fare for the rest of the decade either echoed this dream
or continued to present domestic life as a cozy lark. Rural sitcoms,
such as *Petticoat Junction* and *Green Acres*, continued to thrive, as
did shows about magical powers—*I Dream of Jeannie* and *The
Ghost and Mrs. Muir*, for example. The period between 1963 and
1968, so turbulent in the world outside television, saw the virtual
disappearance of working-class family comedies. Not until 1968 did
ethnicity return to the small screen, with *Julia*, starring Diahann
Carroll as a young, distinctly upscale black nurse who had been
respectably widowed when her husband was killed in Vietnam.
With hindsight, the discrepancies between the social worlds inside
and outside television seem startling, but they caution against
parsing the meanings of television for its "reflection" of lived
experience.

Domesticating the Television Workplace: The Dramatic Series

While the situation comedy was establishing itself as a core of
network entertainment, so too was the other major form of the
episodic series, the hour-long action-adventure drama. Like the
sitcoms, many dramatic series were simply transferred from radio

to television. Their setting, however, was not the home but the workplace, the public sphere, which was largely defined as both male and "professional" territory. In the first half of the 1950s prime-time schedules abounded with police shows (*Dragnet, Gangbusters*) and shows about private detectives (*The Adventures of Ellery Queen, Man against Crime, Martin Kane, P.I.*), establishing the crime drama series as a stock genre of evening television programming. Between 1955 and 1963 the popularity of the crime series was temporarily eclipsed by the Westerns, which occupied eight out of the top ten positions in the ratings for most of this period. From 1958 to 1961 the top three shows were *Gunsmoke, Wagon Train,* and *Have Gun, Will Travel.* Despite the longevity of one or two (*Gunsmoke* remained a favorite until 1972, *Bonanza* until 1971), the Westerns too began to die out after 1963 and were replaced in the top twenty by more contemporary professionals— medical shows such as *Ben Casey, Dr. Kildare,* and, in 1969, *Marcus Welby M.D.,* and legal dramas such as *The Defenders.* There also were science fiction and espionage adventures (*The Twilight Zone, Star Trek, Mission Impossible*) and a scattering of detective and cop shows (*77 Sunset Strip, The Untouchables*).

Despite their immediate roots in radio, the model for both crime shows and Westerns came from movies, a result of the television industry's shift to Hollywood and the increasing involvement of the film studios in television production after 1954. Coinciding with the success of the gangster movies and of "adult" Westerns like *High Noon* and *Shane* in the early 1950s, the networks' experimentation with both forms found ready-made audiences. But if television dramas were cashing in on the established popularity of movie forms, they were also transforming them into more characteristically televisual genres—tamer, more domestic, and more affirmative of emergent mainstream norms.

In film, as John Cawelti (1976) has observed, the Western and the crime movie rehearsed and emphasized the central value conflicts of public life in postwar America: conflicts between tradition and progress, individualism and organization, violence and legal process, freedom and conformity, heroism and the average man. The relationship of movie cowboys and gangsters to modern institutional authority and values had always been adversarial and troubled. Film critic and essayist Robert Warshow

(1979) argued that movie gangsters and cowboys were invariably alienated loners, each in his way at odds with his society and resisting modernity; both were morally ambiguous figures. The movie gangster, wrote Warshow, "appeals to that side of all of us which refuses to believe in the 'normal' possibilities of happiness and achievement; the gangster is the 'no' to that great American 'yes' which is stamped so big over our official culture" (136).

In the television crime and cowboy series the "no" quickly became a "yes." The lawmen of early television series were better-socialized heroes, cleaned up for television by producers so sensitive to the dangers of giving offense to sponsors and the mass audience they courted so eagerly that they could ill afford the negativity and open-endedness of the theater movie narrative. Physical violence was toned down, not merely to meet the anticipated disapproval but also because the small screen restricted the scope for movement so that much of the drama had to be accomplished through talk rather than action. Similarly, the wide open spaces so critical to the visual pleasure of the Western movie, as well as the grimy urban streets and gray waterfronts of the gangster film, had to be scaled down for television or replaced by representative interiors, achieving a more domestic atmosphere.

Many of the themes carried over from film—violence, law and order, professionalism, authority, the return to earlier values— persisted, but television simplified, personalized, and sentimentalized them. The episodic series called for a clear-cut polarization of good and evil, uncomplicated motivation, and narrative closure, generally in the form of a happy ending, or at least one in which the villain got his just deserts. Thus, although television inherited audiences who were familiar with the generic conventions of crime novels and gangster movies, it rapidly reworked the genre, ritualizing the violence and excitement while meeting the real or potential demands of official scrutiny and a huge audience.

In both movies and television the focus on public life and work became also a meditation on the changing meaning of professionalism in modern society. Will Wright (1975) observes a shift in Western films of the late 1950s from the lone hero to the group of heroes. The "professional plot," in his view, called attention to the irrelevance and weakness of social institutions in the collective life of movie cowboys: "The social values of love, marriage, family, peace, and business are things to be avoided, not goals to be won" (85). By contrast the television professionals (policemen, detectives, Western lawmen) came to function as agents of the modern social order. *Dragnet,* the most popular cop show on television in the 1950s, bent over backward to legitimize its preoccupation with violent crime by basing each episode on "real-life" cases drawn from the files of the Los Angeles Police Department ("only the names have been changed to protect the innocent"). Lieutenant Joe Friday embodied to perfection the modern, bureaucratized professional; dedicated but dispassionate ("Just the facts, ma'am!"), patiently digging away at the canker of city crime, case by case. The prevailing tone of *Dragnet* was one of studied objectivity and attention to procedure (statistics, dates, and times were solemnly supplied), setting a precedent for the docudrama style that was rapidly copied by other police shows (*The Lineup, Highway Patrol, Naked City*). And the police always won, legitimizing the rule of law and its representatives.[7]

In the detective show, by contrast, the professionalism of crime control was turned on its head and became glamorous and less routinized, with the police typically portrayed as dull, plodding, or overly bureaucratic. Shows like *Martin Kane, P.I.* and *The Adventures of Ellery Queen,* and later *Perry Mason* and *77 Sunset Strip,* featured maverick sleuths whose brilliant, mercurial intuitions often ignored or circumvented legal process in the pursuit of truth. Taken together, the cop show and the detective mystery may have begun to reflect public ambivalence toward the law and legal authority, as well as toward a more rationalized, universalistic professionalism. Like the policeman, the private investigator always got his man, but with a flashier, more stylish display of virtuoso skills. Each in his own way (and it was always his—women either played subordinate roles, like Perry Mason's secretary Della Street, or were simply absent) possessed a character admirable in every respect, humanized by the lovable foible or the tragic personal loss that left him unattached and therefore devoted to his calling and his colleagues.

As in the sitcoms, the continuity provided by the episodic format shifted the emphasis in the dramatic series from action to character, emotion, and relationship. Since plot structure remained the same from one series or one episode to another, it was the character and

personal style of the central figure, and increasingly his integration
into a group, that became crucial. Mirroring the evolution of the
sitcom, it was the group, the collegial gemeinschaft, rather than the
single star that invited audience attachment. Unlike the ambiguous
heroes of the gangster movie, in the television series neither the
policeman nor the private eye was a loner, dwelling on the margins
of society. Joe Friday had his partners; Perry Mason had Della and
his associate Paul Drake; Stu Bailey had Jeff Spencer and Kookie. In
television drama the crime buster worked within, and was
sustained by, his own professional work group, whose relationships
became so exclusive, so intimate, that they came to resemble those
of the quintessential primary group, the family. In this respect the
dramatic series began to echo the structure and form of the situation
comedy as well as of its concerns. Indeed, as Horace Newcomb
(1974) has observed, the dramatic series took the basic structure of
the television comedy and drew it into the public sphere. The effect
was to create a harmonious, if eccentric, domestic retreat within the
workplace; in television the group came to define both the meaning
of family and the meaning of professionalism.

The same was true of the television Western. From *Gunsmoke* to
Have Gun, Will Travel to *Bonanza*, the Western gradually shed the
alienation that defined its movie counterpart. Where Gary Cooper
in *High Noon* and Gregory Peck in *The Gunfighter* were
world-weary, depressed, and outmaneuvered by the inexorable
march of modernity, *Gunsmoke*'s Matt Dillon became its legitimate
representative, his use of the gun sanctioned by his badge rather
than his honor. For all its celebration of traditional values, the
dramatic series, like the comedy, also welcomed progress. Marshal
Dillon had begun as a fairly typical Western hero, laconic and
solitary, an unwilling killer; but as the series unfolded, his rougher
edges were smoothed off and, together with his family of oddball
associates, Kitty, Doc, and Chester, he came to advertise the values
of a modern pluralistic social order, a benign, legalized justice
tempered with mercy and tolerance. In the shows of the 1970s
those values were to be called into question.

Have Gun, Will Travel's Paladin presented himself as an entirely
more glamorous, but equally modern, figure—the freelancing
cowboy turned streetwise detective. Paladin modernized the
Western into a more urban frame, spending as much time solving

his "clients'" emotional and psychological problems as he did disposing of malevolent wrongdoers. *Bonanza*, the outstandingly popular weekly saga that chronicled the life of an all-male family on its cattle ranch, the Ponderosa, retained the format of the Western in only the most minimal sense. As the series unfolded, the misdeeds of cattle rustlers or lawless killers took a back seat to the developmental problems of Ben Cartwright's sons. More and more *Bonanza* articulated contemporary concerns in the popularized psychological language of the 1960s. Its reassuring domesticity, sentimentality, and championing of tolerance and compassion signaled both the demise of the traditional Western and the roots of the nostalgic rural family drama later to be embodied in *The Waltons* and *Little House on the Prairie*, which painlessly reconciled traditional values of simplicity, decency, and community with visions of progress and modernity.

By 1963 the number of Westerns was dwindling in favor of comedies. Crime dramas too were less numerous, and detective shows seemed to fade out altogether. In the 1961–1962 season two new dramatic series brought the more upscale, modern professions of law and medicine to the television screen. CBS followed its Saturday night showing of *Perry Mason* with another "serious" legal drama, *The Defenders*. Where *Perry Mason* was essentially a detective show with courtroom dramas tacked on, *The Defenders* broadened the courtroom drama format with richer characterization and an underlying discussion of legal and social issues. Here the lawyer appeared less a sleuth than a thoroughly modern but humane protector of constitutional rights and due process.

In the same season the other two networks produced their own successful professional dramas. NBC's *Dr. Kildare* and ABC's *Ben Casey*, the first nighttime soaps, brought the medical profession to the television screen in a highly idealized and sentimental form. The drama came not from social issues but from florid story lines, in which patients died or were miraculously cured of rare diseases that did nothing to diminish their physical beauty, or in which the young doctor's progress, both personal and professional, was threatened by the errors of youthful inexperience. Common both to *The Defenders* and to *Dr. Kildare* and *Ben Casey* was a central relationship between an older and a younger professional, in which the former played father and teacher to the latter, providing the authority—moral and cultural as well as legal or medical—that firmly but gently molded his protégé to fit the requirements of his organizational surroundings. Doctors Gillespie and Zorba were as much psychological counselors and family therapists as they were physical healers.

The fantasies of benign omniscience, omnipotence, and devotion to public service that found repeated expression in these shows glossed over some major tensions in twentieth-century professional-client relationships: the rationalization and bureaucratization of professionals in large organizations, their lack of autonomy and remoteness from the concerns of their clients, and the primacy of rules and profits over service and ethics. All three shows confidently endorsed the ideology of the "classical" or "free" professions: autonomous exercise of specialized skills, concern with ethical issues, and exclusive devotion to clients or patients. Money was hardly mentioned; professional issues shaded off into personal ethical ones, and the two were rarely in conflict. The individual and the group were in harmony with an essentially benevolent society whose legitimate representative was the professional himself. Though medical and legal series have become stock items of prime-time programming, public ambivalence about doctors and lawyers was not to surface in their narratives until well into the 1970s. As late as 1970 Marcus Welby was hammering out the contours of the moral as well as medical universe for his grateful patients and their families.

Differences in generic form shape audience expectations in different ways, but television genres have all been structured, in varying degrees, by the language of realism, which makes the medium a persuasive translator of received ideas into facts of nature. Like all representational narrative, television strives to convince us that its words and images reproduce our own experience or that of people like us. This is partly why people often recall the past in the deceptively innocent language of popular culture (we hark back to a Norman Rockwellian age or to "the fifties"). With its visual naturalism, its attention to the quotidian details of ordinary lives in recognizable domestic and work settings, television has disguised its interpretive character, inviting the viewer to forget that a story is being constructed. The force of that disguise varies from one set of genre conventions to the next. Thus the documentary stakes a claim for more or less absolute fidelity to reality. The docudrama and fact-based made-for-TV movie, which blur the line between fact and fiction, are nonetheless "truer" than the dramatic series. Yet they lack the power of the continuing series to mobilize identification with characters who are "realistic" because they are ordinary folks with plausibly familiar lives that go on "just like ours." (This is one reason why programmers, public interest groups, and media researchers alike are often so concerned that television entertainment should be "realistic.") The sitcom advances itself as more realistic than the caricatures of the Disney cartoon. But comedy is also stagier, more explicitly theatrical, than drama, and it is played for laughs, which lends it the subversive potential of creating divergent readings.

During the first two decades of television entertainment, as I have shown, that subversive potential was held substantially in check. The defining tone of prime-time television during these years was consensual and integrative, reflecting the prevailing political and cultural temper, as mediated by the internal dynamics of an industry addressing itself to a massive, largely unknown audience, and therefore committed to holding the middle ground and avoiding controversy in its construction of the social world. In both drama and comedy, family structures and relationships became a central allegory for social life, whether in domestic or occupational settings. At the same time, the dramatic series revealed the growing salience of ideologies of professionalism, in which the professional provided not only specialized or substantive skills but also psychological, moral, and cultural leadership. Both drama and comedy series overwhelmingly proposed a symmetry between the individual, the group, and a society whose central institutions of marriage, family, business, medicine, and law were conceived as fundamentally benign. The "liberal conservative" spirit of television during these years smoothed out and endorsed the path of progress, bringing its viewers modernity (consumerism, tolerance, and pluralism) wrapped in the traditional values of honesty, simplicity, individual freedom within a protective community, and free enterprise. Just as the family became the cheery social integrator in sitcoms, so the professional work-family painlessly adjusted the individual to the corporate world of the 1960s.

To some degree, then, the stance television adopts toward social

trends has always been influenced by ad hoc changes in the
strategies used by the industry to attract audiences. The powers
that be, who decided in the early 1950s to phase out "ethnic"
sitcoms such as *Amos 'n' Andy, Life with Luigi,* and *The Goldbergs*
and replace them with the upper middle-class coziness of *Leave It
to Beaver* and *Ozzie and Harriet,* may well have thought they were
reproducing the typical American family—if not of the present,
then certainly of the near future—just the people their advertisers
sought to reach. What they reproduced, in fact, was less the
experience of most family lives than a postwar ideology breezily
forecasting steady rates of economic growth that would produce
sufficient abundance to eliminate the basis for class and ethnic
conflict. The "end of ideology" would produce "middle classlessness," a social consensus with the family as the essential building
block, integrating the individual into a benevolent social order.
Thus the Nelsons and the Cleavers were both advertising and
embodying the American Dream.

It is unlikely that such grand visions circulated at programming
conferences in the network entertainment divisions—or if they did,
they percolated through the more immediate, perceived imperatives of the market. From the beginning, producers and networks
made their programming decisions with advertisers in mind. In the
1950s that meant casting nets as wide as possible to deliver a "mass
audience" of potential buyers for the flood of consumer goods and
services that poured off production lines. To fashion a mass out of an
enormous, heterogeneous, and highly mobile population, the
successful network careerist adopted the motto "least objectionable
programming," which produced those least objectionable families,
the Cleavers, the Nelsons, and the Andersons, whose magically
spotless kitchens came amply and strategically stocked with the
latest consumer durables. Taken together, these shows proposed
family life as a utopia transformed by the palpable ordinariness of
television into a plausible, immediate reality; past and future
merged into an eternal present.[8]

As British cultural historian Raymond Williams (1977) has
observed, there are no masses, only ways of seeing masses. By the
mid-1960s the dream of a harmonious, middle-class America united
by material plenty and political consensus was fraying visibly at the
edges. The latent schisms of class, race, gender, and generation

erupted into open conflict. But for the time being, programming executives, for all their declared sensitivity to changes in public mood, stubbornly went on seeing—and producing for—the masses they needed to raise advertising dollars. If television news was, perforce, preoccupied with images of urban unrest, an increasingly volatile economy, the escalating Vietnam War, and a generation of college students rebelling against the values of their parents, the makers of television entertainment blithely pretended nothing was going on—until 1970, that is, when a decisive shift in network ratings policy reshaped the industry's construction of its audiences and created conditions more responsive to the new cultural temper and more hospitable to the emergence of new shows, still powerfully driven by the imagery of family but more combative and critical in spirit.

3

Prime-Time Relevance
Television Entertainment Programming in the 1970s

In the years between 1963 and 1968 television news and entertainment were generating an oddly dichotomous social imagery that both touched on and contrasted with the political and social tenor of the period. Historians pinpoint the assassination of President John F. Kennedy as a symptom of, and a preface to, years of crisis and polarization at home and abroad. The escalation of the war in Vietnam and the slow buildup of the antiwar movement signaled the collapse of a consensus that perhaps had existed mainly in campaign speeches and policy statements—and in television families. At home urban poverty imprinted itself on the public mind in the form of civil unrest and ethnic conflict, shattering the promises of unlimited economic expansion and widespread prosperity that had peppered the speeches of politicians throughout the 1950s and early 1960s. The civil rights movement splintered, in the face of waves of racial unrest, into more militant factions of black, Chicano, and Native American interest groups. Environmental groups challenged corporate rhetoric about the unalloyed benefits of industrial expansion, raising issues of health and safety in the workplace as well as the consequences of automation—higher unemployment and routinization of the blue-collar and expanding white-collar sectors.

The women's movement began to dig a steady, subversive path into the consciousness of both men and women, shaking up long-cherished assumptions about sex roles, marriage, and family life and demanding equality of pay and opportunity in the workplace. The emergent divisions of race, gender, and class were filtered, in the media, through the prism of youth and family. Since young people—especially, though not exclusively, college students—were the most visible dissidents, "youth culture" began to be perceived by social scientists and cultural critics as a major organizing category of contemporary American culture.[1] The media fastened on the "generation gap," the conflict between parents and children, to explain social conflict in both the domestic and the public spheres, and its primacy tended to obscure more long-standing tensions.

In entertainment, as I have shown, the television narrative either suppressed these conflicts or expelled them symbolically to an external world perceived as autocratic, hostile, and threatening. The news media could hardly ignore what was going on, and during this period nightly news shows presented viewers with a world routinely filled with problems, confusion, and ominous events. Still, television news coverage continued for the most part to support government policy, with the result that social conflict was not so much neglected as polarized into good and evil, silent majority and lunatic fringe.[2] The same was true for coverage of the Vietnam War, which became through the medium of television, in a phrase coined by television critic Michael Arlen (1982), America's first "living room war." Through the middle years of the 1960s little doubt was cast by the news media on the legitimacy of American policy in Indochina (Hodgson 1976).

Opposition to the war and to government policy, both domestic and foreign, grew more vocal in the later years of the decade in the thriving alternative media and among sections of the public at large, particularly among disaffected university groups, the active centers of the New Left and the antiwar movement. In 1968 Martin Luther King, Jr., and Robert F. Kennedy were assassinated, and in the same year President Lyndon Johnson announced he would not seek another term in office. The decisive break in news media support for United States government policy came with Walter Cronkite's CBS News report on his return from Vietnam, in which he suggested that the United States might have to accept a stalemate in Southeast Asia. In August at the Chicago Democratic Convention journalists as well as protesters took a literal beating at the hands of Mayor Richard Daley's police. The alliance between government and media shifted, with the news media taking up a watchdog role of moderate opposition that was shortly to be echoed in entertainment themes.

In 1969 the tone of prime-time entertainment also began to shift, signaling in its own way the collapse of the "end of ideology." Although the episodic series, framed in the imagery of family, remained the dominant television genre, both comedy and drama moved away from the consensual mood of the 1950s and 1960s toward a more abrasive style and more open confrontation with contemporary social issues. The turn toward "relevance," as the trend was called among network executives, grew out of a complex interplay between, on the one hand, emergent social and cultural trends and, on the other, more immediate pressures for change in ratings and programming strategies within the industry itself. Indeed, it was largely as a new marketing device that the turbulence of the middle to late 1960s and the adversarial spirit of the generation coming of age during this period found their way into the genres of television entertainment.[3]

The networks' earliest attempts at "relevance" were clumsy and short-lived. In 1968 ABC's *Mod Squad*, an attempt to cater to the youth market while retaining the attention of older audiences, featured three young social outcasts—"one black, one white, one blonde," as the ads went—who were roped in to act as undercover agents for the Los Angeles Police Department. In 1970 CBS made its own bid for the attention of "the counterculture" with *Headmaster, The Interns,* and *Storefront Lawyers*. At this stage "relevance" meant peppering the scripts with hip language presumed to characterize the argot of youth, and the action with drug culture and political subversion; none of the shows lasted long (Castleman and Podrazik 1982).

In the same year Bob Wood, the incoming president of entertainment at CBS, undertook an extensive overhaul of his network's programming strategy. Wood realized that although CBS was the number one network in raw ratings, its most successful shows (*Gunsmoke, The Beverly Hillbillies, Hee Haw*) appealed primarily to older, rural viewers and rated less well among younger, more upscale audiences in the cities. Wood also saw that from the point of view of advertising sponsors what mattered was less *how many* people tuned in than *how much* they earned and were willing to spend on consumer products. These insights, together with his perception that younger, more affluent, urban social groups were fast becoming if not numerical then cultural leaders, prompted

Wood to revise his ideas about targeted audiences and shop around for program ideas that would "fit" the new markets. The name of the new ratings game was "demographics," which meant breaking down the mass audience by age, sex, income, and other sociological variables that would isolate the most profitable sources of revenue—namely, urban viewers between the ages of eighteen and forty-nine, especially women, who remained the chief buyers of consumer goods for themselves and for others in their families. Accordingly, scheduling became an elaborate strategic exercise whose purpose was no longer merely to reach the widest possible audience with any given show but to group programs and commercials in time slots by the type of audience likely to watch (and spend). The purpose was not to dismantle the mass audience but to fine-tune it, focusing on its most lucrative segments. Thus it was that the themes of youth, in television if not in everyday life, were played out within and reconciled with the theme of family. Throughout the 1970s and 1980s television advertising has reflected the same trend toward specialization of markets within the mass audience, with commercials carefully orchestrated to draw specific demographic groups in appropriate time slots while retaining advertising geared to the whole family.

These shifts of perspective on audiences awakened Wood and CBS chairman William Paley to innovative programming suggestions that departed from existing formulas and led the network entertainment division into a fruitful alliance with several independent production companies, notably Norman Lear's Tandem and Grant Tinker's MTM Productions, and with veteran comedy writer Larry Gelbart. Their work for CBS, together with the refinement and sophistication of television programming and marketing, would quickly establish a new style of comedy, modifying and extending the genre, articulating with particular shifts in public consciousness while producing commercially successful products, and setting the tone for prime-time entertainment throughout the 1970s and early 1980s.

That tone was influenced primarily by three comedy series that formed the backbone of CBS's highly successful Saturday night lineup. The first, MTM's *The Mary Tyler Moore Show*, a comedy about a single woman in her thirties taking up a career at a minor Minneapolis television station, picked up a substantial and loyal following among viewers for the next seven years (not to mention its long and continuing life in syndication). Among them, perhaps, were the same fans who had so adored Moore in her role as Laura Petrie in *The Dick Van Dyke Show*. In January 1971, thanks again to Bob Wood, the new series was joined by Norman Lear's *All in the Family*, a comedy whose pilots had twice been rejected as too controversial by ABC. The show, based on the enormously successful British television comedy *Till Death Us Do Part*, depicted a white working-class bigot, Archie Bunker, angrily confronting a new era of liberal pluralism through a ceaseless war of words with its youthful advocates, his "progressive" daughter and son-in-law (the latter was, all too appropriately, a sociology student). The program was a slow starter in the ratings, taking a full sixteen weeks to get off the ground, but Wood was patient and stuck it out, protecting Lear from the censoring hand of network executives fearful of alienating both viewers and sponsors. His tenacity was rewarded when *All in the Family* climbed into first place in the ratings and remained there for five years.[4] In 1973 these two hits helped nurse along another CBS hopeful, *M*A*S*H*, which, when sandwiched between the other two in the Saturday night lineup, leaped into the top ten and remained there until its demise in the early 1980s. Based on the 1970 Robert Altman movie about an army medical unit surviving the Korean War, *M*A*S*H* combined a moderately antiwar position with a "war-is-fun" wackiness that was likely to draw in younger viewers with widely varying political perspectives in the aftermath of the Vietnam War.

A woman, single and attractive but no longer in the first flush of youth, struggles to forge a career and a new personal life in a corporate world dominated by men. A working-class conservative nurtured on blind patriotism, xenophobia, and respect for hard work, family, and paternal authority finds his most cherished beliefs challenged first by his offspring, then by his wife; eventually he suffers unemployment, impotence, his daughter's divorce, and a host of other social problems that erode his domestic haven. An army medical unit stumbles through a war whose purpose is far from clear and whose military leadership commands at best an ambivalent allegiance. What set these shows apart from most of their predecessors was their topicality for audiences in the 1970s, a topicality refracted through the defining lens of the news media. All three were centrally concerned with rapid social change and its attendant normative dislocations, the daily confusion thrust on ordinary people (as opposed to the glamorous undercover agents and streamlined advocates of *Mod Squad* and *Storefront Lawyers*) facing puzzling and often painful new conditions without adequate rules to guide their actions. Each dealt in its own way with the crisis of styles of authority—personal, occupational, political—grown arbitrary and irrelevant, whose legitimacy was constantly called into question; and each worked out the "newer" concerns of younger generations within the more traditional frame of family. The concerns expressed by cultural critics, described in Chapter 1—the crisis of authority in both private and public life, the divisions of gender, age, race, and class—were finding their way into the discourses of television, mediated by the commercial exigencies of the industry as well as by broader changes in consciousness, in which, of course, the media had a shaping hand.

For viewers there were both old and new satisfactions. In many ways the new shows were firmly rooted in the conventions of traditional situation comedy, relying on absurd escapades or misunderstandings uncovered or resolved by the end of each episode. *M*A*S*H*'s bouncing repartee recalled the rapid-fire banter of standup comedy and of earlier army comedies like *The Phil Silvers Show* and *Hogan's Heroes*. Archie Bunker's blustering pratfalls and malapropisms echoed those of Ralph Kramden and Chester Riley. Sweet, accommodating Mary Richards stepped out of the chrysalis that had contained Laura Petrie. The familial structure of the sitcom, whether at home or in the workplace, remained as fundamental as ever; with or without a central star, the force of the shows came from the interactions between the group members. But there were also significant changes of style and mood. Humor in the new shows was more verbal and less dependent on action than that of previous sitcoms. No longer were these comedies filled with the happy mirth that resounded through the houses of the Cleavers and Nelsons, those advertisements for the American Dream. If mirth and solidarity were anywhere to be found, it was more likely to be in the growing numbers of series with workplace settings. What viewers could see in story after story was individuals negotiating, in a muddled, haphazard sort of way, increasingly familiar troubles and surviving them with a cheerful, if bemused, resignation.

TABLE 2. *The Rise of Relevance: Changes in Top-Rated Prime-Time Programs, 1968–1974, Ranked by Audience Size*

Nielsen Averages through 4/2/69		Nielsen Averages through 5/8/74	
1968–1969	*% TV homes*	*1973–1974*	*% TV homes*
Laugh-In (NBC)	31.1	All in the Family (CBS Tandem)	31.2
Gomer Pyle, U.S.M.C. (CBS)	27.1	The Waltons (CBS Lorimar)	27.9
Bonanza (NBC)	27.0	Sanford and Son (NBC Tandem)	27.6
Mayberry R.F.D. (CBS)	25.8	M*A*S*H (CBS Gelbart)	25.8
Family Affair (CBS)	25.2	Hawaii Five-O (CBS)	23.7
Julia (NBC)	25.1	Sonny and Cher (CBS)	23.4
Gunsmoke (CBS)	24.8	Maude (CBS Tandem)	23.3
Dean Martin (NBC)	24.1	Kojak (CBS)	23.3
Here's Lucy (CBS)	23.7	The Mary Tyler Moore Show (CBS MTM)	23.2
Red Skelton (CBS)	23.6	Cannon (CBS)	23.0

Source. Erik Barnouw. 1975. *Tube of Plenty: The Evolution of American Television.* New York: Oxford University Press.

Resolution came less from a misunderstanding revealed, a situational asymmetry set to rights, than from a continuing process of social learning, a wobbly accommodation to new conditions of living without clear-cut rules or figures of authority.

It would be rash to infer the cultural temper of a decade of television from three comedies, but by 1973 the innovations pioneered by CBS were fast becoming a formula. Copying successful programs and scheduling strategies had long been routine in television entertainment. Now a new technique, the spinoff, speeded up the crystallization of new generic forms. Characters thought to have won audience affection were "spun off" into their own series. *All in the Family* generated its own family of similar shows: *The Jeffersons, Maude,* and *Good Times* in the 1970s, *Archie Bunker's Place* and *Gloria* in the early 1980s. From *The Mary Tyler Moore Show* came *Rhoda, Phyllis, The Nancy Walker Show,* and eventually *Lou Grant.* Trapper John of *M*A*S*H* was spun off into his own hour-long medical drama, and when *M*A*S*H* ended its final run in 1982, it produced the short-lived *Aftermash.* Not only characters but also occupations, themes, or relationships perceived as having "taken" among audiences were reproduced by the same production companies and then swallowed up by others, with the networks' blessings.

Out of this continuous process of splicing and copying—what Todd Gitlin (1985) calls the "recombinant culture" of television—emerged new strains of television drama and comedy. By the 1973–1974 season the new CBS shows and their spinoffs had captured most of the top ten positions in the Nielsen ratings, giving an overall picture vastly different from that in 1968–1969. *All in the Family* topped the charts, with its spinoff *Maude* doing well at number seven. The only NBC show to make it into the top ten was another Norman Lear creation, *Sanford and Son,* inspired by a British series about two junk collectors, *Steptoe and Son,* only now with a black cast. *M*A*S*H* placed fourth, and *The Mary Tyler Moore Show* ninth. The evening lineup of shows tailored for particular markets, pioneered by CBS, was to become a key element in network scheduling wars in the 1970s and 1980s.

Although "relevant" comedy was clearly the centerpiece of the new programming philosophy, other developments were also represented. In second place in the ratings was *The Waltons,* a brand-new hour-long drama chronicling the lives of a Depression-era rural family. Also in the top ten were three new police-detective dramas, *Hawaii Five-O*, *Kojak*, and *Cannon*, all from CBS, which set a precedent for more sophisticated, urbane action shows in which the lines between good and evil, heroism and villainy, grew steadily more ambiguous. Only *The Sonny and Cher Hour* (also from CBS) retained the variety format; but this was decidedly hip, up-to-the-minute variety—abrasive, rooted in popular music, and clearly aimed at younger audiences. Thus the first half of the decade saw the consolidation of "relevant" programming, with the other networks rushing to copy CBS's most popular formulas. Of the independent companies now dominating production, Tandem and MTM Productions were much in demand, and they were joined by other companies, notably Lorimar and Spelling-Goldberg Productions, in the race to produce social issue–oriented pilots for the major networks.

So it was that commercial criteria helped modify existing television genres without making them unrecognizable to viewers. In comedy—still easily the prime-time favorite—two patterns took shape, extending, recontextualizing, and dichotomizing the family metaphor so deeply embedded in television entertainment from the beginning. Following *All in the Family*, shows with domestic settings tended to be overwhelmingly about troubled families—divorced or single parents, fractured or reconstituted families, families full of conflict. Among the few shows with "intact" families were *The Waltons* and *Little House on the Prairie*, both hour-long dramas rather than comedies, and both vehicles for nostalgia modeled on *Bonanza* and harking back to a romantically refurbished small-town past. Comedies with workplace settings, such as *The Mary Tyler Moore Show* and *M*A*S*H*, tended to be only secondarily about work; their central characters and relationships looked, felt, and sounded like the idealized families we carry around in our heads, equipped with the emotional loyalties, intimacies, tensions, and supports associated with mid-twentieth-century kinship ideals.

Among action-adventure series, police and detective shows made a comeback, multiplying across the schedules of all three networks. The formula of violent street crime resolved in favor of law and order was retained, but here too there were significant changes. Gradually the glamor of international intrigue and espionage of the cold-war era was abandoned in favor of more "ordinary" murder and robbery in the city streets around the precinct. The Vietnam War was coming home in more ways than one. Police officers and detectives were idiosyncratic and quirky (Kojak, with his bald head, his lollipops, and his predilection for flashy suits; tubby Cannon; dilapidated Columbo) but rarely handsome in the muscular Hollywood manner. If they were, it was often tongue-in-cheek, like the shambling, bashful Jim Rockford. Recalling the determined realism of *Dragnet*, set designs emphasized urban grime and decrepit offices instead of gleaming tile and creaseless uniforms. The villains in these shows were more likely to be highly placed professionals (doctors or lawyers) or corporate executives than lunatics or street criminals. And although most crime dramas revolved around a single star, the hero operated from within the work-family that had germinated in the action-adventure series of the 1950s and 1960s. Far from being shadowy background figures, Kojak's colleagues—McNeil, Crocker, Stavros, and Saperstein—evolved into highly individuated characters with specific roles more familial than occupational in nature.

By the middle of the decade, then, "relevance" had established a firm hold on the character of the episodic series and set a pattern that persisted in prime-time programming into the 1980s, consolidated by the wide range of 1970s shows available as syndicated reruns. The topical concern with media-sanctioned social problems and events also found its way into new television genres that sprang up alongside the episodic series. Made-for-TV movies, a lucrative new line produced quickly and relatively cheaply and featuring well-known television stars, tackled problems like juvenile delinquency, child abuse, mental illness, rape, anorexia, divorce, and other "women's issues," situating both problem and resolution within the family, however troubled (Taylor and Walsh 1987). The enormously successful miniseries *Roots, Holocaust,* and *QB VII* addressed racial issues and endorsed ethnic pride. Within the episodic series, the docudrama *Lou Grant* built plots around environmental pollution and government corruption.

"Relevance" threw into sharp relief the tendencies toward a social problem–oriented didacticism that had been present in television from the beginning. Because of its near-universal

TABLE 3. *The Age of Relevance: Top-Rated Prime-Time Television Programs, 1974–1975, Ranked by Audience Size (September 1974–April 1975)*

	Program	Network Rating			Program	Network Rating
1.	All in the Family	CBS	30.2	14.	Kojak	CBS	23.3
2.	Sanford and Son	NBC	29.6	15.	Police Woman	NBC	22.8
3.	Chico and the Man	NBC	28.5	16.	S.W.A.T.	ABC	22.6
4.	The Jeffersons	CBS	27.6	17.	The Bob Newhart Show	CBS	22.4
5.	M*A*S*H	CBS	27.4	18.	The Wonderful World of Disney	NBC	22.0
6.	Rhoda	CBS	26.3	19.	The Rookies	ABC	22.0
7.	Good Times	CBS	25.8	20.	Mannix	CBS	21.6
8.	The Waltons	CBS	25.5	21.	Cannon	CBS	21.6
9.	Maude	CBS	24.9	22.	Cher	CBS	21.3
10.	Hawaii Five-0	CBS	24.8	23.	The Streets of San Francisco	ABC	21.3
11.	The Mary Tyler Moore Show	CBS	24.0	24.	The NBC Sunday Mystery Movie	NBC	21.3
12.	The Rockford Files	NBC	23.7	25.	Paul Sand in Friends and Lovers	CBS	20.7
13.	Little House on the Prairie	NBC	23.5				

Source. Tim Brooks and Earle Marsh. 1979. *The Complete Directory to Prime Time Network TV Shows 1946–Present.* New York: Ballantine Books.

Note. In the mid-1970s all but three of the top twenty-five shows were episodic series: seven were domestic comedies, two were domestic dramas; four were workplace comedies, nine were workplace dramas.

availability and its location in the home, public interest groups have always placed television under greater pressure than other entertainment media to be "socially responsible," especially where family issues are concerned. It is ironic that a medium so frequently derided or dismissed as "junk" is nonetheless subject to closer monitoring of its moral and social content than any other popular cultural form. At least in their public rhetoric, practitioners, critics, and watchdogs of television often seem to treat the medium more as a public relations tool than as a mode of artistic expression or even of entertainment. The commitment to a social and moral pedagogical role, especially on the part of vocal producers like Norman Lear and Larry Gelbart or actors like Alan Alda and Ed Asner, helped legitimize "relevance" in entertainment programming and, in time, turned television into the most self-consciously sociological of the media. But it also exposed the networks to the scrutiny of influential interest groups with their own definitions of what was "responsible," "relevant," or, indeed, "realistic," as well as what was "pro-family."[5]

It was partly because of the industry's sensitivity to public opinion that, in 1975, the tide began to turn away from "relevance." The most immediate cause was network fright at the growing influence on the FCC of lobbying groups opposed to "excessive" sex and violence in television. Early that year the National Association of Broadcasters took the initiative and censored itself by establishing Family Hour, a nightly hour of programming between 8:00 and 9:00 P.M. that was allegedly purged of material deemed offensive to children and other vulnerable groups. The ruling did, at least for a while, restrain more explicitly violent or sexual shows, but it also succeeded in banishing from the small screen in peak viewing hours many of the topical comedies and dramas so carefully nurtured during the early years of the decade, severely damaging their ratings potential.

After a flurry of short-lived family shows (the only lasting innovation was NBC's *Little House on the Prairie*) and a successful suit brought by Norman Lear and other top producers against the NAB in federal court, the networks were prohibited in 1977 from continuing Family Hour. But the networks had backed themselves into a corner; they could hardly retreat from a measure designed, as they had loudly proclaimed, to protect children. The initiative came from Fred Silverman, newly defected from CBS to the weaker ABC and one of an emerging breed of college-educated network programming executives, who turned the restrictions of Family Hour to his own advantage. Building on his new employer's strengths by revamping existing youth-oriented and family shows like *Happy Days* and developing others that would accommodate the exigencies of Family Hour, Silverman also acquired a reputation for scheduling wizardry by playing around with the time slots to maximize ratings. ABC was catapulted back to prominence with nostalgic, consensual comedies like *Happy Days* and its spinoff, *Laverne and Shirley;* comedies with modern settings but traditional, slapstick formats, such as *Three's Company* (based on the British hit *Man about the House*), or stand-up comic banter, such as *Welcome Back Kotter*. Superhuman powers returned to the action-adventure series with *The Six Million Dollar Man* and its spinoff, *The Bionic Woman,* and to comedy with *Mork and Mindy*. Taken together, these series seemed to be announcing the death of the counterculture, "normalizing" youth by stripping away its oppositional edge and integrating young people into families; *Happy Days*'s Fonzie was literally domesticated by his adoption into the middle-class Cunningham family. Yet even in these more conventional series, television's treatment of family was skittish. *Happy Days* was a nostalgia vehicle set in the 1950s. *Mork and Mindy* turned family roles on their head, with the childlike alien Mork married to the girlish but maternal Mindy, and their union producing an adult-size child. And *Three's Company,* with its three roommates (one man and two women) dancing nervously around the norms of dating, sexual orientation, and relationships, offered an anxious commentary on the ambiguities of the single life.

If the first half of the decade could be called the CBS years, the second half might well be labeled the ABC years. In action-adventure, the prolific Spelling-Goldberg duo turned out two gimmicky new police series—*Charlie's Angels*, ostensibly a show about three young policewomen but actually an excuse for sexual titillation and ersatz violence; and *Starsky and Hutch,* much the same thing only with two male stars. ABC also aired Spelling and Goldberg's *Family,* an hour-long drama somewhat in the mold of *The Waltons* but more contemporary, chronicling the lives of a stable California couple whose older children nevertheless confront all the familiar troubles of divorce, single parenthood, death, and other "relevant" problems.

The ABC hits did for a while succeed in edging out the Tandem and MTM shows from the top ratings slots, but the urbanity and social-problem orientation that developed in the first half of the 1970s remained a feature of prime-time programming and established themselves as core characteristics of television entertainment in the 1980s. Although Norman Lear's company has not produced a lasting hit comedy in the 1980s, the treatment of prominent social issues is now firmly entrenched in the domestic comedy of that decade. In drama, too, the first half of the decade brought great success to MTM Productions with sophisticated one-hour dramas like *Hill Street Blues* and *St. Elsewhere*, produced for NBC. Indeed, these shows helped boost the network's flagging fortunes by building on the conventions of "relevance" and repackaging them as "quality television" (Feuer et al. 1984).

Between 1969 and 1972, then, the tacit and explicit rules governing production routines and programming decisions shifted ground, and new kinds of judgments about what would sell and what was culturally significant hardened into everyday practice. The longer view, backward into the 1950s and forward into the 1980s, suggests as much continuity as change in the restless oscillations of television entertainment. Over time, genres acquire stable characteristics with all the inertia of institutionalized habit. The formal structure of the episodic series remained familiar: segments built around commercials, continuity provided by the ensemble of characters, and repetition of plot and situation. Within the traditional frames of home and work, however, old problems surfaced in new ways. Although television has from the beginning been the most sociological of popular media, the significance of "demographic" ratings strategies was that they created a space for a spirit of criticism, a forum for more open and genuinely adversarial public discussion than had been possible in earlier decades when the search for a mass market had, it was thought, required the creation of a normative consensus. Changes in substance shaded off into changes in form, in particular a tendency toward greater structural ambiguity, the eliding of drama and comedy, more unresolved endings, and greater complexity of character. It is not surprising that the collapse of the television consensus worked itself out more in comedy than in the dramatic series. The potential always present in comedy for generating a dissident voice was liberated by commercial imperatives, by the search for symbols that would appeal to a young, liberal, upscale audience making the transition from turbulent college campuses to the workplace. Liberated up to a point—since that dissidence was also held in check, contained by the simultaneous need to sustain the attention of a broader mass audience conceived as more mainstream in its values.

The fluctuating fortunes of "relevance" might be read as just part of the cycle of television faddishness. The television industry operates on the principle of ongoing, frantic, short-range competition, and "relevance" grew out of network competition for the attention of viewers—in the case of CBS, an effort to stay ahead of the game and retain its dominant position; and in the case of ABC, a temporarily successful attempt to pry itself out of last position. In this instance, though, the guesses of Bob Wood and others were confirmed by the ratings, and their guesswork was soon hallowed as professional knowledge.[6] According to the Nielsen ratings, audiences obliged by watching the new shows over a sustained period of time. Indeed, to judge by the ratings of the CBS Saturday night lineup and its clones on other networks, the "relevant" shows were drawing in mass audiences much as their predecessors had done in the 1950s and 1960s. But programmers were focusing on those segments of the market that they perceived as potentially most attractive to advertisers and hiring producers whose work, in their judgment, addressed their presumed concerns and public attitudes. It was this kind of thinking that shifted the sensibility of television programming from liberal-conservative to liberal-pluralist.

It is plausible that Lear, Brooks and Burns (of MTM), and Gelbart were, in their different ways, better equipped than other producers to put their fingers (however inchoately) on critical points of tension and change in American culture at that moment in history.[7] Producers vary in the degree to which they perceive the success of their shows as the direct outcome of the messages they intend them to convey. Norman Lear, a producer openly committed to expressing political and social values through his comedies, declared himself skeptical about the power of television to bring about general attitudinal change, but he believed that specific effects could be achieved:

I don't believe at all that it [*All in the Family*] reinforces *anything* bad in society. But again, I don't see that it has changed anything for the good, either. I would be a horse's ass if I thought that one little situation comedy would accomplish something that the entire Judeo-Christian ethic hasn't managed in two thousand years. But there have been some specific results, results that were measurable. This usually occurred when we did a show on such a subject as clear and specific as health.

(quoted in Newcomb and Alley 1983, 193)

The spinoff device established for Lear and a small number of other production companies a reputation for success that brought them more work and greater freedom from network supervision and allowed some of them to develop a distinctive "house style." Thus Lear's company became known for its belligerent dialogue with current social and political problems at the national and international levels, while MTM Productions developed series with a quieter, more subtle "relevance," scaled down to the exploration of character and interpersonal relationships. Although Lear's primary goal was to entertain his viewers, he had little doubt that the topicality of his comedies, the critical confrontation with media-sanctioned issues—generational conflict, racism, sexism, civil rights and freedom of speech, corruption in high places—were as responsible for their popularity as their humor. In 1979 he told the *Boston Globe*:

I've had a strong conviction for some time that you can discuss national issues and deliver a large audience if it's done just right. . . . I want to do SALT and nuclear energy and right-to-life and other issues that trouble people. . . . People will watch. And they will learn. You get warmth and fire by rubbing things together.

(*Boston Globe*, September 3, 1979)

By contrast, James Brooks and his collaborator on *The Mary Tyler Moore Show*, Allan Burns, felt that their success derived from the creation of plausible characters rather than trendy issues:

I think that the difference between our style and Lear's, for instance, is that he probably would have made a big deal of Mary's sex life. He deals with controversy; we are subtler about it. . . . We dealt with problems, the day-to-day stuff that ordinary people go through as opposed to big themes that Norman would take on: birth control and abortion. Our issues were the small ones. . . . Despite the fact that there is a large war going on, basically those are people just trying to get through the day.

(quoted in Newcomb and Alley 1983, 215)

Still, for all their mistrust of polemic, Brooks and Burns acknowledged the inseparability of character and broader topical concerns in their writing. As Brooks observed of *The Mary Tyler Moore Show:*

We didn't want to say that American life was perfect, trouble free. . . . *I mean our timing was very fortunate* [emphasis added], the way the women's movement started to evolve. So not only our ideas, but what was happening in society began to appear in the show. But we did not espouse women's rights, we sought to show a woman from Mary Richards' background being in a world where women's rights were being talked about.

(quoted in Newcomb and Alley 1983, 219)

According to Todd Gitlin, who interviewed more than two hundred members of the Hollywood television community in 1981, producers and network executives get their information from the same sources as the public at large—from relatives and friends, but most of all from the mass media themselves. Norman Lear told Gitlin:

We all get our stimuli from the same wellspring. . . . It's exactly the same, wherever you are in this country. We all read whatever we read— *Time* or *Newsweek* or whatever. . . . They're all the same, the big newspapers. And that's where we feed, writers. We feed and drink from those wells.   (quoted in Gitlin 1985, 204)

In his essay on the Lear comedies, television critic Michael Arlen attributes Lear's success to the growth among the general public of a national culture based on this hectic "media consciousness," which he identifies as

the commonality that seems to have been created largely by television itself, with its outpouring of casual worldliness and its ability to propel—as with some giant, invisible electric utility feeder line—vast, undifferentiated quantities of topical information, problem discussions, psychiatric terminology, and surface political and social involvement through the national bloodstream.

(Arlen 1976, 64)

Thus producers both absorbed and helped create a cultural climate that legitimized certain themes as significant and interpreted them in particular ways. Network executives proceeded with their scheduling and programming decisions as if social issues were the recipe for ratings success. They may have been correct, but all they had to go on were high ratings, which established only that a large number of viewers tuned in to these shows and suggested almost nothing about *why* they watched, or indeed *what* these shows meant to audiences, or *how* viewers were engaging with television.

The relationship between producers, the images they create, and audiences is diffuse, unpredictable, and mediated by the complex structure of the industry. Viewers' engagement with television remains opaque partly because their tastes are filtered through the flattening statistics of Nielsen ratings. In any case, most producers acknowledge that their immediate audiences are not viewers but the networks (who finance production), and, through them, the sponsors. This dependency on network approval, mediated by the bottom line of ratings, creates for the most successful production companies a highly uncertain (if lucrative) working environment. It discourages risky innovation even among the small group with substantial "creative clout" and may account for the diplomatic but ambivalent tone taken by many producers when they talk about the networks.[8] James Brooks, whose work on *The Mary Tyler Moore Show* was unusually well protected from network interference by Grant Tinker, chief executive at MTM Productions, nonetheless cited this difficulty as a major reason for not forming his own production company:

Competing with all the other pilots that are made to get on the air in a season is not an atmosphere that produces good work. . . . The line between producing and hustling becomes very blurred. It requires saying, "They'll like this and this will test better." It involves acceptance of a lowest common denominator, a certain unflattering view of the audience and a callousness.

(quoted in Newcomb and Alley 1983, 210)

Television, described again and again by creators as a producer's medium, is a collaborative process (Norman Lear's company employed a total of between seventy-five and one hundred staff when *All in the Family* was in production, and at any given time he was overseeing the simultaneous production of several shows). Many producers find the cooperative aspects of production satisfying; indeed, the domesticity that pervades the television series, whether set in homes or workplaces, may in part mirror the working conditions of television creators:

[Television] is warm and when it's working that surrogate family . . . is not only on the screen, it's part of your life. There is something about coming in for five or six years and doing good work with the same people day in and day out—it's a terrific environment.

(Brooks, quoted in Newcomb and Alley 1983, 223).

Some producers, searching for more direct and spontaneous interaction with viewers, try to include them in that surrogate family through the practice, pioneered in the early 1970s, of taping an episode before a "live" studio audience and then intercutting that episode with previously taped versions. But the final recourse to tape suggests an ambivalence toward the reactions of an unknown, and therefore uncontrollable, entity.

Thus viewers are seen by producers through the dark glass of a hierarchical and diffused decision-making process, as well as through the reductive operations of ratings. Indeed, it is likely that network executives are reluctant to receive audience information that is too specific. For all their interest in demographic breakdowns, they must still show advertisers evidence of mass viewing for their shows.[9] In this sense commercial television production embodies to perfection the tensions of mass-produced culture. Like it or not, those who create television shows are accountable to the interests of networks and sponsors, and to the degree that they must try to create a huge, undifferentiated audience for their products, the ideas and images they create tend to hug the normative middle ground and mute the minority or dissident voice in favor of a populist consensus.

At the same time, since neither producers nor viewers are a "mass" but are a heterogeneous—and stratified—collection of groups and individuals, the meanings of television must embrace at least the rhetoric of pluralism and speak to the central divisions of class, race, age, and gender that shape public consciousness. The mass audience programmers had sought to reach in the 1950s and 1960s could be conceived only as consumers; on no other grounds, cultural or political, could they plausibly be lumped together. In the early 1970s, in order to target the demographic groups within that mass offering the most commercial potential, programmers had first to identify them as distinct political and cultural entities and to craft programs for them without in the process alienating or losing the rest of the audience. To this end controversy and youthful concerns were played out in that most "normal" of institutions, the family, which frames the experience of everyone and pulls marginal or dissident imagery toward the reassuring center of universal experience, the apparently extrapolitical realm of private life.[10] The topicality of the "relevance" formula may well have succeeded precisely because its issues were grounded in television's prototypical figures—ordinary people living in families.

Audience response is elusive, then, not just because of the reductive ways in which the industry collects information but also because there is no such thing as "the audience." Understanding the relationships between producers, meanings, and audiences has proved as vexing a problem for scholars as it has for television executives and ratings companies. The audience in media studies, as Michael Schudson (1987) has remarked, "has been (like the weather) something that everybody talks about and nobody does anything about" (60). In part this is because media scholars spent many years trying to find ways to expand and refine a model of "media effects" that echoed market researchers' efforts to pinpoint clear-cut messages in television that had observable impact on the attitudes and behavior of viewers. Though quick to demonstrate the shortcomings of ratings systems, only in the 1980s have social scientists turned a critical eye on their own methods and begun to develop more sophisticated and dynamic models of mass communications that link audiences *actively* both to the messages of television and to the work of production.[11] Building on the perspective of uses-and-gratifications research, scholars are turning the effects model on its head and asking not how media messages affect audiences but how media are integrated into the everyday lives of viewers of all kinds. How is viewing shaped by social location in the divisions of class, race, age, and gender? How do viewers see television in general in relation to other narrative forms?

Thus far, as is usual when new paradigms emerge, conceptual advances in audience research have outstripped empirical studies, which remain scanty. The few audience studies carried out in the 1970s indicate that viewers' interpretations of television interact with the beliefs and conditions of their own lives, a conclusion that supports a more complex view of audience response. As a more substantial body of empirical work emerges, attending to the ways in which viewers appropriate and integrate what they see on television, we become more aware of the dynamic, varied roles of television viewers—and of the shifting, multiple meanings of television.

Between producers and viewers lie the programs—the stories of television or, as Clifford Geertz (1973) has put it, the "imaginative works built out of social materials" that explain a society to itself. The value of a flexible textual reading, one that looks for a range of shifting meanings in television and examines *how* television language invites its viewers to appropriate particular meanings, is that it avoids the assumption of a narrow, linear causality between on the one hand, either producers' intentions or definitive "content" and, on the other, a monolithically conceived "audience reaction." A central insight of the cultural studies approach is its reading of popular culture as socially constructed and received.[12] But if the challenge of cultural studies is its grasp of the television narrative as social practice *and* as artifact without abolishing the connectedness of making and receiving television, this insight also raises the conceptual and methodological difficulty of a dynamic analysis, one that makes the links, or realizes the *dialogue*—as Newcomb (1984), following Bakhtin, calls it—between different moments in the communication process. Anthony Giddens (1979) observes that "one of the main tasks of the study of the text, or indeed cultural products of any kind, must be precisely to examine the divergencies which become instituted between the circumstances of their production, and the meanings sustained by their subsequent escape from the horizons of their creator or creators" (44).

That escape is the subject of the following two chapters. The meanings of television are made in particular contexts, but they are no more reducible to technical structure or production routines than any other cultural form. As Chapter 2 showed, they grow away from the intentions of their creators and become objectified as programs and genres with shifting, multiple meanings and are "read" in many different ways by viewers. As Richard Johnson (1986–1987) observes, "Processes disappear in results" (46). We cannot *directly* infer the meanings of television from the conditions of its production, or vice versa. Nor can we equate the meanings constructed by viewers watching television for entertainment or escape with those of the media critic working within the frames of academic or journalistic convention, or with those of a producer working within the organizational exigencies of the television industry, though the range of disparity will be limited by the cultural boundaries that audiences, critics, and producers inhabit through a common language.

The lack of a codified orthodoxy in cultural studies permits a useful embrace of precisely this tension between what Johnson calls the "culturalist" emphasis on historical processes of production and reception and the "structuralist" analysis of forms and meanings. The interdisciplinary approach of cultural studies encourages the researcher to pay attention to the interstitial areas and to move between them in the work of analysis. Taken together, these two attitudes can produce a "structural ethnography" of meaning in television, something akin to Geertz's (1973) notion of "thick description." In Chapters 2 and 3 I have tried to render explicit the social practice of network television and show how marketing and organizational procedures, as well as assumptions about salient social issues and viewers' tastes, shaped the development of television genres and their changing imagery of work and family from the 1950s to the 1970s. Chapters 4 and 5 move to a detailed interpretive analysis of that imagery during the years of "relevance." A close reading of the programs themselves, informed by what we know about changing conditions in television production and reception, digs beneath the surface, single-issue realism of "media consciousness" to deeper themes and concerns about social change in public and private lives. In the shows of the 1970s the concerns of cultural critics about family and workplace described in Chapter 1 are echoed and transformed by the particular language of network television.[13] In a period when family and workplace, and the boundaries drawn between them, are rendered problematic, television calls attention to family distress. Thus the meaning of family is recast and becomes the framework for new kinds of social conflict—not only the well-publicized tensions of race, gender, class, war, and so on, but also conflict about the family itself. Anxiety about changes in family life—in the nature of authority in both the public and the private spheres—carves a deep fault line through the imagery of prime-time programming in the 1970s. The form, nature, and symbolic resolution of this anxiety is clarified in the following detailed discussion of individual shows and the genre of the episodic series as a whole.[14]

4

Trouble at Home

Television's Changing Families,
1970–1980

In the 1970s, as I argued in Chapter 1, public attention was focused on changes in family structure, in particular on domestic distress. The television family in this period echoed these concerns, in sharp contrast to the relative harmony, unity, and integration within the wider society of television families in the 1950s and 1960s described in Chapter 2. Helped along by the self-conscious preoccupation with social problems of television producers committed to "relevant" programming, the 1970s television family became a forum for the articulation of social conflicts of all kinds. The vast majority of series with domestic settings offered viewers troubled or fractured or reconstituted families. These domestic dramas reflected the anxiety about the erosion of domestic life that was beginning to punctuate the rhetoric of politicians and policymakers, social scientists and therapists. From the more visible problems like spouse or child abuse, divorce, and teenage pregnancy to the less tangible areas of marital conflict, social trouble was increasingly being defined as family trouble. But if this picture suggests parallels with cultural criticism and ethnographic work on the family, nevertheless the television narrative *reworks* the concerns of the 1960s and 1970s within its own genre conventions, such that not only "private" troubles but also the "public" problems of youth, class, race, and gender are drawn into the family frame, converting the domestic sphere into a febrile and argumentative war zone.

Television, as has been shown, has always spoken the language of family in both its themes and forms—the realist visual and verbal codes that one sees not only in the individual show but also in the highly recombinant and formulaic episodic series. The domestic

comedy that provided the backbone of prime-time entertainment
from the beginning continued through the 1970s. In the 1974–1975
season seven out of the ten top shows in the Nielsen ratings were
domestic series (six were comedies and one was a dramatic series).
Of these, five came from Norman Lear's production company,
Tandem/TAT Productions, while MTM Productions contributed
Rhoda, a successful spinoff from *The Mary Tyler Moore Show.*
Nowhere were the public debates of the late 1960s and early 1970s
more self-consciously aired than in Lear's domestic comedies,
which set the cultural agenda for other "relevant" shows by bringing
to the fore the divisions of race, gender, generation, and (more
weakly) class and recasting them as family problems. The "age of
relevance" in television was ushered in by *All in the Family* and
speeded up by the spinoffs and copies it generated across the
prime-time schedules of all three networks. The Bunkers, and in
their wake the Jeffersons and the Findlays (*Maude*) and the
Romanos (*One Day at a Time*), quarreled, stormed, and suffered
their way through the 1970s, blazing a trail for the array of social
problems that became the standard fare of television families. The
following discussion offers a reading of the ways in which the "house
styles" of the Lear and MTM series, as well as the "family drama"
series, reshaped public images of the domestic and the relationship
between the family and the outside world.

Of all the prime-time shows of the 1970s, *All in the Family* stands
out as the best known. Aside from the enormous audiences it drew
throughout the decade, in 1971 the show carried off several Emmy
Awards and established a name for itself as the best new situation
comedy of the year.[1] Critics waged wordy struggles over its merits
and weaknesses on the pages of the *New York Times* and the *Los
Angeles Times* as well as in the tabloid press. Social scientists
conducted surveys into the impact of Archie Bunker's bigotry on
adult and juvenile audiences (Meyer 1976). Literary critics and
cultural commentators analyzed the program and its social significance at length (Lasch 1981). Lear and his ensemble of actors
were interviewed, praised, and attacked, not only about the show,
but also about their political views. Bill Moyers devoted two full
episodes of his *Creativity* series on public television to the work of
Norman Lear. And in 1978 *All in the Family* was officially enshrined

in cultural history when Archie's chair was installed in the Smithsonian Institution.[2]

All in the Family was not the first television show to experiment with topicality. As I showed in Chapter 2, the anthology dramas of the 1950s relied heavily (if less self-consciously) on contemporary social problems for their story lines. In the 1960s dramatic series like *The Defenders* and *East Side, West Side* also spoke to current concerns of civil rights, poverty, and inequality, while satirical shows like *Laugh-In* and *The Smothers Brothers' Comedy Hour* drew extensively on prevailing political and social controversies. Several features distinguish *All in the Family* from its predecessors. First, its shock value: the show sounds different from previous family comedies. Its central character is an unrepentant bigot whose speech is peppered with racist epithets—"hebes," "krauts," "coons." Archie's bluster is more topical than Ralph Kramden's ever was. Second, the quantity of earnest explanatory publicity that accompanied the show's debut lodged it firmly in the minds of its creators, the networks, the sponsors, the FCC, and the critics, if not the viewing public at large, as a new form that dealt seriously with current social issues. In television aesthetic value, to the extent that it is considered at all, often translates as "social responsibility" or "realism." Because of its topicality *All in the Family* was received as a creative innovation.

Initially audiences appeared to greet *All in the Family* with some indifference, but it generated much heated discussion among critics and cultural commentators in the mainstream media who (whether or not they liked the show) accepted it, in the spirit of its creators' intent, as an attempt to debate significant public issues of national concern within the framework of entertainment. With few exceptions critics fastened on the racial and political aspects of the show as central. Amid the furious debate the show's success was defined—if not by the mass of viewers, then certainly by opinion leaders—in terms of the manner in which it addressed current affairs. If Lear was not the first to extract humor or drama from social conflict, he was the first to construct a situation comedy around it.

All in the Family is, like most television comedy by the end of the 1960s, a family chronicle, whose action unfolds in the Queens home of Archie and Edith Bunker, a middle-aged, white, working-class couple; with them live their daughter Gloria and son-in-law Michael, a Polish American. Unlike its antecedents, however, this family is constituted as a forum for waging the ideological battles of the Nixon era as seen by Lear and his stable of writers. In early seasons especially, plot and character are typically built around the received political polarities constructed in the news media. A 1971 episode sets the tone for the ceaseless cycle of quarreling and abuse between Archie and Michael, whom he calls Meathead. Michael and Gloria's first anniversary dinner becomes the occasion for a flashback to Michael's first meal in the Bunker household. Ignited by a television news item announcing the arrest of two hundred protesters in an antiwar demonstration, Michael and Archie polarize and goad one another about the meaning of patriotism:

> *Archie:*   Here in America—the land of the free where Lady Liberty holds her torch sayin', Send me your poor, your deadbeats, your filthy . . . so they come from all over the world pourin' in like ants . . . like your Spanish, your P.R.'s from the Caribuan, your Japs, your Chinamen, your Krauts and your Hebes and your English fags . . . all of them free to live together in peace and harmony in their own little separate sections where they feel safe, and break your head if you go in there. That there is what makes America great!

Michael in turn outlines his own brand of national loyalty: "I love it too, Mr. Bunker . . . and it's because I do that I protest when I think things are wrong." He challenges Archie:

> *Michael:*   You sayin', America, love it or leave it?
> *Archie:*   That's right . . . it's a free country, so *am-scra!*
> *Michael:*   But what would our leaving solve? With or without protesters we'd still have the same problems.
> *Archie:*   What problems?
> *Michael:*   The war. The racial problem. The economic problem. The pollution problem.
> *Archie:*   Aw, c'mon, if you wanna nitpick!

Edith's efforts to mediate bring about a brief truce, but an ostensibly innocent discussion about baseball blossoms into a full-scale row, in which Archie's racial prejudices get their usual strident airing:

Archie:	Yer coloreds, as is well known, run faster, jump higher, they don't bruise so easy . . . because of their, what you call it, their jungle heritage, they see better . . . great for night games!
Michael:	I did misjudge you. You're even more ignorant than I thought!
Archie:	You are one dumb Polack!

With this exchange the battle lines are drawn and the ideological parameters set for a struggle between Archie and Michael (Gloria siding with her husband) that repeats itself innumerable times in subsequent episodes of *All in the Family*. It is a conflict between generations in which social problems are lined up like ducks on a shooting range and argued back and forth in a contest between tradition and modernity, the liberal conservatism of the post–Vietnam War decade and a new version of progress defined as liberal pluralism, with the moral weight firmly skewed toward the latter.

In each conflict it is not ultimately Michael who thwarts Archie (plenty of fun is poked at the trendy young sociologist too) but the plot, hacking away at his mulish intransigence. The typical narrative pattern has Archie outmaneuvered in one of several ways. His wily, intricate schemes to cheat the Internal Revenue Service, defraud an insurance agent who is also an old friend, or capitalize on a new device invented by a Jewish acquaintance all end in disaster. His conservatism, rehearsed in blustery malapropistic tirades against feminists ("you female libertines!") regularly leaves him nursing verbal wounds inflicted by those more in tune with social progress, more skilled than he at the small diplomacies of modern interaction. His knee-jerk bigotry invariably lands him in situations that confront him with the objects of his prejudice, whose dignified refusal to be rattled or harassed make him look stupid. "How'd you like the *Julia* show yesterday?" he asks his black neighbor Louise Jefferson by way of self-introduction. "How'd you like *Doris Day?*" she retorts without batting an eyelid.

Archie is an absolutist marooned in a highly relative, ambiguous social environment he can no longer effectively read. In episode after episode he is bludgeoned by his encounters with the brave new modern world, always in situations ripe for social learning. But he never learns; he may be stymied or even briefly cowed (his unlikely alliance with a Jewish vigilante bent on violent reprisal ends, in one of those jerks out of the comedy format that came in later seasons to define the show, when the vigilante is blown up by a bomb planted in his car by an anti-Semitic group), but he returns with each new episode to scheme and rail and vilify. The other characters, by contrast, adapt more readily to change. Gloria "deserts" her father, first by marriage to a liberal, then through upward mobility when her husband becomes a professor of sociology, and by the birth of her own energetic feminism. Even Edith, his staunch defender, learns to assert herself, goes out to work, and begins to disagree with him when she feels he is wrong. Archie wages an eternal losing battle against the inevitabilities of change, and more and more he wages it alone, without allies.

Archie's primary agenda is his loathing for the vocal emergent minorities of the 1960s—ethnic minorities like blacks, Jews, and Hispanics—as well as homosexuals, feminists, civil rights activists and gun control advocates. But he also hates the police ("The cops can't find a big guy like Jimmy Hoffa . . . how they gonna find her?" he sneers when his adopted daughter Stephanie is reported missing), the Internal Revenue Service, the church, the corporations, indeed the state itself—all the large institutions (except his union) that govern his life and threaten the shopworn dream of a society founded on the labor and loyalty of hardworking small entrepreneurs, to which he clings so tenaciously. Indeed, the threat is material as well as ideological; insecurity plagues his job at the docks, and finally he is laid off, becomes a janitor, then a cab driver, then a bartender, and ends by buying the bar from his boss (the bar becomes the setting for *Archie Bunker's Place*, the early 1980s spinoff from *All in the Family*).

Archie represents a class culture at bay, dispossessed by a brash, pluralistic world he comprehends only dimly but will fend off to the death. "They'll think I'm one of those Park Avenue dudes with money to burn," he complains when Edith puts on her Sunday best to accompany him to the Internal Revenue Service. And he tells the implacable IRS auditor, "See, I'm only a little guy. Now I ain't one of your big corporations, can run down to H & R Block whenever they got a problem." Yet he clings, against all the evidence, to the rags-to-riches mythology on which his generation and his class were reared. "D'you honestly think you could make half a million dollars in your lifetime?" asks Michael, exasperated for the thousandth time by his father-in-law's political myopia. "Why not?" replies Archie, "It's a free country . . . it could happen!" And his newly acquired color television set carries a weighty symbolism: "Y'know, there's about three great moments in a man's life . . . he buys a house, a car, and a new color TV . . . that's what America's all about!" The trouble is that he is wrong: these precious goals no longer are what America is about. Archie is precisely the disenfranchised patriarch whose demise Christopher Lasch was to lament in *The Culture of Narcissism* and feminists applauded. Archie's fulminations against women, Jews, blacks, and other minorities add up to a long bellow of pain from a man whose most cherished guidelines for living—family, country, authority—have been pried loose by the relentless rush of modernity.

In each episode the plot, with Archie as the fall guy at its center, serves as a concrete illustration of a social issue, bounced around by the dialogue at a high level of abstraction. "You men treat us like unpaid servants!" complains Gloria, newly won over to feminism. "That is nothing but a male chauvinist attitude!" Archie, threatened by the arrival of a black family (the Jeffersons) next door, grumbles, "These people are movin' up in life and we're movin' down." "Archie, they've done sociological studies on this," remonstrates Michael, "the socioeconomic status of those who move in is higher than that of the original inhabitants." But it is Edith who innocently supplies the more biting social commentary. "Only two years ago they was servants. Now they're doctors and lawyers. They've come a long way on TV!!"

Plot and dialogue, then, are openly didactic. The moral and political dice are loaded in favor of Lear's well-publicized liberalism, leaving little room for interpretation. Yet the limited data on audience reaction to *All in the Family* indicates that the lives and values of the Bunkers were appropriated to shore up widely divergent attitudes and beliefs (Vidmar and Rokeach 1974). Timothy Meyer's (1976) study of the show's impact on children found that the moral and political concerns of *All in the Family* took a back seat to character as a source of identification.[3] Of the children interviewed, 44 percent liked Archie best and 25 percent liked him least, in both cases for the same reason: "Archie yells at Edith when she acts stupid." Being funny, looking good, and being nice were more crucial qualities than "doing what is right." These admittedly limited findings suggest that viewers become involved at least as strongly with character as with plot and that they respond to themes other than, or in addition to, the political or ethical lessons intended. To get at some of these themes requires a search for patterns of narrative, character, formula, and other generic characteristics—the language of the text not immediately available to us through its manifest concerns.

For all Norman Lear's reputation as an innovator, the formal structure of his comedies is traditional. In many ways *All in the Family* is the quintessential sitcom, full of the pratfalling physical comedy found in *I Love Lucy, The Honeymooners,* or *The Life of Riley* and in the vaudeville routine. Archie and Michael regularly get stuck trying to get through the same doorway. Michael drops a hammer on his foot; Archie delivers a Bronx cheer or contorts his face into the familiar, overstated grimace when he is disgusted or outwitted. The flushing toilet and lavatory jokes are constant routines. Character, action, and interaction have the stiff, unchanging quality of the cartoon. Each is defined by exaggerated physical or verbal quirks: Archie's grimaces, his epithets (Edith is a "dingbat," Michael a "meathead"), Edith's awkward, enthusiastic run, her tuneless singing, Gloria's blonde, doll-like good looks. To judge by the timing of the "live" audience laughter, it is precisely the predictability of their stock responses to stock situations that appeals. Relations between the characters have the undifferentiated belligerence of the Punch-and-Judy show, each raining verbal blows and counterblows on the others' heads, with Edith as the beleaguered buffer.

Lear's comedies typically end with a proud voice-over from one of the cast, "This show was videotaped in front of a live studio audience," implying that studio audience response is more spontaneous than the canned laughter used in filmed shows. Any account of viewer response, however, must consider the fact that videotape creates even more possibilities than film for splicing and editing; though the laughter, the clapping, and the heckling are "real," they can be moved around, intensified, muted, or eliminated. Moreover, Lear was known, in the early series, for appearing in front of a studio audience and warming them up before taping began. Often an episode was taped several times, with variations, and the "best" version used.

All in the Family is also formulaic in new ways. Each character is representational in a more modern sense, informed by the "media consciousness," the pop-sociological and pop-psychological sensibilities of the newer audiences, that Michael Arlen (1976) discerned. The Bunkers offer us a television commentary on well-known and culturally resonant social types: the working-class Republican, the nurturant, slightly daffy but intuitive wife, the radical young sociologist, the new feminist. In Lear's comedies characters tend to represent social issues, and the relationships between them argue out the tensions between tradition and modernity, between women and men, and between generations, classes, and ethnic groups.

What lies behind the ideological debate, and what may just as plausibly have engaged the interest of viewers, is the mood of anger itself, the undifferentiated fury and more muted ambivalence that prevail in the Bunker household. In contrast with the jolly harmony of television families in the 1950s and 1960s, *All in the Family* brings the war, indeed all America's wars, back home. The family remains as powerful an organizing idea as ever in television, but its meanings begin to change significantly. This family has become a stage for the dramatization of conflict; Lear's parade of media-sanctioned, "relevant" conflicts shades into a more generalized ambivalence about social change. Beyond this grows a pervasive sense of unease about the survival of the family itself and its relationship to an outside world increasingly experienced as threatening rather than benign—simultaneously remote and incursive. If Lear and his associates explicitly endorse modernity, celebrating the freedoms and protections it brings the individual, the tone and language of the show as a whole betray an insistent undertone of unease and apprehension. Modernity appears at best a mixed blessing, at worst a material and normative morass. Michael and Gloria tug and pull Archie into the 1970s, he digs in his heels with the defensive truculence that gives the narrative its static circularity. No one gives way, and everyone is angry most of the time.

If Archie offers us the image of a class in eclipse, he also, by extension, represents the demise of the hearthside despot— autocratic patriarchy in decline. His attacks on the women's movement and his desperate attempts to assert his authority as husband, father, and definitive interpreter of the world fall increasingly on deaf ears. He is either challenged or, worse, ignored, as Gloria and Michael struggle to establish a more egalitarian mode for their marriage, and Edith an independent life for herself. For a while the family survives and is reaffirmed as a haven of sorts, the only remaining place where Archie's bigotry, conservatism, and free-floating rage can be let loose without attracting consequences more severe than the indignation of his children. And Edith and Archie's fundamental loyalty to each other and to the institution of marriage remains the bedrock on which the situational and ideological struggles rest.

Over the years the show shifts its focus, moving from "macrorelevance" to "microrelevance," dwelling less on public debates about government and institutions and more on issues defined as belonging properly to the private sphere. Trouble still abounds, but it is articulated as personal or family trouble. Edith grows more assertive and forges a life separate from the world she shares with Archie. She is plagued by a host of "women's problems"— menopause, suspected breast cancer, rape. Gloria and Michael move to California, separate, and eventually divorce. The family is replenished in its final season with the arrival of Stephanie, unwanted daughter of Edith's alcoholic cousin Floyd. Archie himself becomes preoccupied with problems of aging, ill health, and impotence—problems that, as so often happens in television, are nobody's fault and therefore leave him speechless. Illness punctuates the narrative; Archie undergoes an operation for gallstones, a spot is discovered on his liver, he becomes briefly addicted to tranquilizers when business problems plague him in the bar he takes over from owner Kelsey, who suffers a heart attack. Death and the fear of death stalk the show as an ominous theme; Edith's friend Beverly is murdered, Archie's business partner Bernstein collapses and dies in the Bunkers' living room. Several episodes end with a stunned, protracted silence that stands in sharp contrast to the show's habitual clamor and tidy resolution. Finally Edith herself dies, signaling the end of the series and of the Bunker family.

In later seasons it is as though public life is being squeezed further and further into the private sphere, where it becomes difficult for the Bunkers—and their viewers—to identify the roots of private troubles in public life. The change in the show's concerns is accompanied by a shift in tone. Alongside the jaunty aggression of the earlier seasons grows a darker, more alienated mood, less savvy and cocky, more anxious. The feisty battle of wills and ideological posturing becomes a state of siege; the protagonists are less sharply defined, less personalized, and more nameless. A deepening confusion pervades the development of character and narrative, a sense that the family fabric is weakening, invaded first by public institutions, then by arbitrary forces—illness, aging, and death— over which it has little control. Often episodes are grouped together for a full week, allowing a more gradual exploration of particular themes.

All in the Family maintains its topicality but begins to express it in a different register. The raising of gender issues suggests less a considered feminist consciousness (Gloria's shrill textbook feminism hovers around caricature and becomes almost as much a target for audience derision as Archie's resistance) than a formidable sexual confusion, a normative promiscuity mixed with fear of the unknown. Both couples feel obliged to reevaluate the quality of their sex lives on more than one occasion. Impotence crops up twice—once when Michael is worried about an exam and again, more enduringly, when Archie is laid off.

Edith's female relatives and friends present an astonishing range of sexual and marital variation. Her cousin Amelia's "perfect marriage" ends in divorce. Another cousin, the independent Maude, has been divorced three times. When her cousin Liz dies, it transpires that she was a lesbian and has left her estate to the woman she lived with. At a family gathering Edith discovers that her "cousin" Roy is not really a blood relative when he makes a pass at her. A transvestite and female impersonator becomes the focus of several episodes: Archie administers mouth-to-mouth resuscitation to him in his cab; he becomes Edith's friend; he is brutally murdered. Edith and Gloria become (separately) victims of attempted rape, in Edith's case the attempt occurring in her own home while the rest of the family awaits her arrival next door to celebrate her fiftieth birthday. Archie almost succumbs to an affair, jeopardizing the show's most enduring relationship, his marriage to Edith. As *All in the Family* draws to a close, there no longer exists *a* nuclear family, only a multiplicity of primary relationships trying to define themselves.

Underlying the mounting gravity of *All in the Family's* tone is a significant shift in the generic techniques employed to express conflict. In earlier seasons trouble emerges through comedy itself, which serves both to express and contain it. In later series the comedy strains so hard against its own boundaries that it bursts them altogether and often becomes undiluted melodrama. Comedy and drama are also juxtaposed, and the most serious issues are signified by one-hour specials (Edith's rape, her reconciliation with Archie after his "affair"). What begins as food for humor grows too grave for jokey banter, too diffuse for simple plot resolution. The show ends, not with the couple settling into a wiser, more tranquil old age, but with Edith dead, Gloria and Michael far away and separated, and Archie alone with Stephanie—the Bunker family splintered and fragmented.

The force of *All in the Family* is reducible neither to its producers' intentions nor its manifest themes. Undoubtedly the series's topicality played its part: *All in the Family* is firmly embedded in the major public debates of the Nixon era, and it is unlikely the show would have found as large an audience in 1950 or 1960, or for that matter in 1980. But for all its brazen racial epithets, the show was hardly the radical departure from prevailing social norms that the rhetoric in the negotiations between Norman Lear, Bob Wood, and the rest of the CBS establishment implied. Lear emerged as pioneering radical, Wood as protective patron, and the network as cautious overseer. It quickly became clear, however, that there was no real conflict of interest; "relevance" sold, which was enough to satisfy all the parties concerned. Together with its companions in the CBS Saturday night lineup (*The Mary Tyler Moore Show* and *M*A*S*H*), *All in the Family* was merely voicing a slightly modified political orthodoxy—liberal pluralism, respect for the individual and for civil rights, and love of progress tempered with traditional values, all spiced with contemporary sociology and therapeutic language.[4]

In its latent themes *All in the Family* was indeed a landmark. The conjuncture of, on the one hand, Lear's gift for skimming off key tensions in early-1970s culture and parlaying them into mass entertainment and, on the other, a network grown receptive through its revised marketing strategies propagated a show whose changing themes, both manifest and latent, evidently resonated with the concerns of millions of viewers. Lear's programs transcended his intentions, altering the generic form of television comedy and redefining the tenor of conflict to accommodate new kinds of audiences, whose urbane (if superficial) sophistication was informed substantially by the media themselves. Out of *All in the Family* came a whole slew of "relevant" family comedies, defining the house style of Lear's company and spreading among his imitators, that drew and capitalized on contemporary anxieties about family life and acknowledged a diffuse, helpless anger before the disruptive forces of rapid social change. *All in the Family* pioneered a formula for domestic comedy that turned Norman Lear's Tandem Productions into the television success story of the early 1970s, inspiring many imitations along the way. Lear's company produced 25 percent of the top fifteen shows in the Nielsen ratings between 1971 and 1978 and won six Emmy Awards for the 1977–1978 season. His shows legitimized the concern with social problems in television entertainment; from child abuse to the arms race, scarcely an issue under debate in the national culture produced by the burgeoning information industries escapes mention in a Lear comedy. The trend spread, not only in sitcoms, but also in dramatic and action-adventure series and made-for-TV movies. But the key social divisions of race, gender, and, more implicitly, class emerge as central organizing principles for setting, plot, and character development—framed, as always, within the family.

The anxiety, anger, and ambivalence in *All in the Family* are extended with particular force in the three "black" comedies, *Good Times* (1972), *Sanford and Son* (1972), and *The Jeffersons* (1975). Together they made Tandem Productions famous for restoring blacks and other minorities to the small screen after two decades of virtual embargo. Racial inequality had become a major feature of

political discourse throughout the 1960s with the rise of the civil
rights movement, and this, together with the growing interest of
advertisers in black consumer markets, guaranteed some prominence to ethnicity on the list of "relevant" topics for the new
television entertainment. A spinoff from *Maude*, *Good Times* has
Maude's black maid Florida moving back to a high-rise apartment
in Chicago and negotiating the vicissitudes of ghetto life with her
husband James and children J. J., Thelma, and Michael.

Poverty, street violence, and unemployment make routine
assaults on family life in *Good Times*, yet the self-deprecating,
offhand humor that expresses them trivializes their significance. A
characteristic episode illustrates how the family's financial problems become fuel for a string of disclaiming one-liners. J. J. as usual
cannot find a job ("Mr. Evans, is there any reason you're not
working full-time?" sniffs an insensitive adjuster; "Yeah," grins J. J.
agreeably, "I don't have a job"), but now the Evanses face eviction
("We better set the floor for dinner") and must sell the only thing
they own outright, the television. "Ma," groans Michael, "do we
have to sell the TV tonight? I wanna watch *The Waltons!*" "If we
don't sell it," his mother replies, "we gonna *be* the Waltons!" Every
attempt to master their situation ends not only in failure but as often
as not in humiliation: J. J. is mugged in the elevator and the
television, whose sale was to have paid the rent, is stolen. While the
family's solidarity projects the philosophy of cheerful survival that
marks television's new brand of optimism in the face of adversity,
the constant frustration of its goals lends a vindictive, knowing
cynicism to the narrative, a gratuitous cruelty compounded by
J. J.'s grimacing, jive-talking buffoonery, his willing collusion in
others' attempts to make him look stupid: "Hey ma, the kid and I
put our heads together, and now his head's together just like
mine!"[5]

In J. J. we find a tendency that begins with Archie Bunker and
grows more and more pronounced in Lear's comedies: the character, dialogue, or joke that simultaneously evokes and parodies
racial and cultural stereotypy, drawing in the viewer to feel either
identification or contempt, or both at the same time. Do viewers
laugh *with* J. J. caricaturing the urban black teenager or *at* him
because they think he is the caricature? Perhaps both; the
ambiguities in dialogue and performance feed the ambivalence of

the viewer, fostering that peculiarly modern temper of relativism that may help explain why the episodic series has generated so few unambiguous heroes, heroines, or villains since the early 1970s and why unresolved endings have grown more frequent in both comedy and dramatic series.

Lear's other 1972 hit, *Sanford and Son*, plays incessantly on this uncertainty. Like *All in the Family*, *Sanford and Son* is modeled on a British sitcom (*Steptoe and Son*) whose central premise, the daily struggles of a father-son team of junk dealers (fighting with each other as much as with the outside world), is recast as the story of a black duo in the Watts district of Los Angeles. The claustrophobic set for the show, the Sanfords' living room, is stuffed with the flotsam of other people's cast-off lives; in the midst of visible poverty, Sanford implores his son to be careful with the Chippendale. Here, too, we are being invited to laugh sympathetically *with* the Sanfords, or *at* their pathetic attempts to achieve grandeur, or both.

Essentially a series of short skits built around one-liners delivered by Sanford (played by Redd Foxx, a veteran of vaudeville), *Sanford and Son* owes more to *Amos 'n' Andy*, to the ethnic joke, and to vaudeville banter than to contemporary situation comedy. This series gives us an all-black world peopled by lovable, childlike simpletons held in check by tolerant relatives. The senior Sanford is not merely ignorant ("Othello? A black man with an Italian name?") and earthy ("Know what's wrong with this house?" he whispers to his son as they enter the home of a wealthy white family in Beverly Hills, "Ain't got no smell!"); he is also, like Archie, a loudmouthed bigot (he hates "honkies," not so much because they discriminate against him as because they are not black) and a misogynist. We may laugh at him as much as we want, but he is always forgiven because he's such a dear old thing.

A spate of misunderstandings convinces Sanford that his son Lamont is gay; he has been seen going into what Sanford, with a suggestive wave of the hand, refers to as a "sissy-bar" (gusts of laughter, prompted or not, from the studio audience). The doctor (a bumpkinish cartoon figure with the ignoramus's air of grave wisdom) is called in to examine Lamont and, parodying received psychology, asks if there was a "dominant mother." When Sanford goes to the gay bar to investigate further, he too is seen, and Lamont begins to suspect his father is gay. Matters are quickly resolved when each displays, to the other's visible relief and inviting ours, his date for the evening. Order is restored by the affirmation of their heterosexuality. Once again, it is unclear whether the audience cheers or derides Sanford's prejudices or is simply relieved that the world has returned to normal.

The success of *Good Times* and *Sanford and Son* led to the introduction in 1975 of a third "black" comedy, *The Jeffersons*. Like *Maude*, *The Jeffersons* was a direct spinoff from *All in the Family*. George Jefferson, the "pushy black" who moved in next door, made his pile in dry cleaning, and took up residence in an opulent apartment on Manhattan's fashionable East Side, was an eternal irritant to Archie. Here he is Archie's obverse, his mirror image in black; he echoes Archie's personality and family role—aggressive, bigoted, blustery, sustained by his capable, intelligent, kind, and open-minded wife Louise, and forever at odds with a television world that has left behind the defensive separatism to which George clings and has embraced both racial pluralism and racial integration. His son Lionel maintains a close friendship with Michael and Gloria and marries Jennie, the black daughter of George's neighbors Tom and Helen, a mixed-race couple with a "white" son. Louise, gregarious and likable, draws an outside world of whites and blacks alike to their household and remains loving but undeterred by George's loudly voiced opposition.

Like Archie, George lets his self-interested but inept scheming and obdurate prejudice continually plunge him into trouble from which he is bailed out, usually by Louise or Lionel, and taught a moral lesson about means and ends, which he then claims as his own victory. He displays the same infantile, reactive volatility and unfocused rage, the same conniving instrumentality, as Archie, and as with Archie, we are required to forgive him because underneath it all there is a feeling heart. The difference between them is one of class rather than race. George has "made it"; he is rich, and that gives him social power. Where Archie takes cover in the plodding belligerence of the dispossessed, George is a strutting popinjay, striking attitudes and trying on the habits of the wealthy and influential for size. Upward mobility is a central theme in *The Jeffersons*, as the title tune indicates: "We're movin' on up to the

East Side / To a de-luxe apartment in the sky / We finally got a piece of the pie!" This in contrast to the title song of *All in the Family*, with its wistful nostalgia for a lost past.

> Mister we could use a man like Herbert Hoover again
> Didn't need no Welfare State
> Everybody pulled his weight
> Gee, our old Lasalle ran great
> Those were the days.
>
> Title song, *All in the Family*

George's project is to use his economic clout in whatever way necessary to gain his own ends. He is forever signing property deals or throwing largesse around to impress or manipulate others. Ironically, the only person willing to collude with his posturing is Ralph, the obsequious white doorman ("Ah, sir! My favorite tenant!"). At home George is at best tolerated, at worst ridiculed, not least by Florence, the black maid, who, with her ready backtalk and steadfast refusal to perform menial tasks, acts as a permanent thorn in his flesh. George has bought his way into the social world of the rich, and though he is willing to mimic their life-style, he cannot or will not absorb their norms and etiquette, responding with a graceless gaucherie or a dogged belligerence that appears to send the studio audience into transports of delight. Again there is the ambiguity: do we laugh with him as he thumbs his nose at the rich, or at him as he gets above his station?

If anger and aggression pervade Lear's other comedies, in *The Jeffersons* they are raised to the pitch of hysteria. Like Archie, Edith's cousin Maude, and Fred Sanford, George is furious by definition, especially on matters of race. A conflict arises over Lionel and Jennie's wedding; Tom and Helen want it classy and elegant, George flashy and riotous, Lionel and Jennie quiet and unpretentious. "I ain't havin' my son married by no honky minister!" screams George, "I want a black preacher!" He asks the white Baptist minister who unobtrusively performs the ceremony, "You ain't by any chance part black, are you?" If whites are fairly disgraceful, miscegenation is, in his view, beneath contempt. "I have a heavy test tomorrow in black history," confides Jennie, mulatto child of a mixed marriage. "Oh, well," says George with his

satanic grin, "you should get half of it right!" But it is not only race
relations that inspire rage in George. Anger is his habitual stance;
the world is there to be battered into submission.

Lear's shows are designed for family viewing, and their explicit
message is the celebration of family. For this reason, as well as more
obvious censorship considerations in a medium with a mass
audience, physical violence is rare. Yet the language is saturated
with symbolic violence. An episode of *Good Times* has the
neighbors gathered in Florida's living room to discuss solving the
problem posed by a violent local youth gang, the Junior Warlords,
and one man illustrates his remedy by placing a small object (which
he designates as the gang) on the coffee table and smashing it with
a large book. There is laughter and wild applause from the
audience. "Mr. Parker," says Florida, "we are concerned parents,
not vigilantes. We wouldn't have any gangs if parents took
responsibility for their own kids," for which she receives a decorous
if unenthusiastic clap from the studio audience. It is clear that while
they find her position unexceptionable, it satisfies them much less
than Mr. Parker's more confrontational solution.

On one level Norman Lear's ethnic comedies are clearly meant
to explore the black (and other minority) experience and examine
the complexities of black-white relations in a changing world,
where minorities have achieved formal recognition as equal citizens
but remain victims of prejudice and economic oppression. They
also offer a clear-cut moral woven into the plot structure and usually
personified in a woman; namely, that honesty, integrity, kindness,
and social responsibility always pay, while deviousness and
mean-spirited behavior are doomed to ignominious failure. Yet that
message contrasts sharply with, and is effectively undercut by, a
ubiquitous language of concentrated (if undiscriminating) violence
and aggression. This may be a major source of the tremendous
appeal of Lear's comedies. They bring together and reconcile
multiple, often contradictory kinds of satisfaction. Parading before
us a host of topical contemporary debates, they extol the virtues of
the freedoms provided by progress and modernity and encourage
us to endorse a liberal orthodoxy of tolerance, pluralism, kindness
to others, and good citizenship. These values, of course, have
always been part of the diffuse, unthreatening humanism that
pervades a medium dedicated to not giving offense. But the Lear

series also give voice to public ambivalence and confusion about precisely these issues and beliefs. If Archie, Maude, Fred Sanford, J. J., and George and their perpetual battles with the world provide a critique of cultural stereotyping, they also *embody* the caricature, allowing us to laugh in several directions at once. The Lear comedies pander to a uniquely contemporary style of laughter— nervous, politically and morally insecure, open to manipulation, and, above all, angry.

The same skittishness pervades the family imagery in these shows. Lear's ethnic families are formally "intact" in the sense that they have not been compromised by the commonest contemporary source of dissolution—separation, divorce, and abandonment. Fred Sanford is a widower, Florida Evans becomes a widow halfway through *Good Times,* and in both cases we understand that their marriages were happy. Like most television comedies, they declare their allegiance to family values and family unity. This is particularly true of the Evanses in *Good Times,* whose huddling together in adversity recalls the warm solidarity of *The Goldbergs* and *Life with Luigi.* Still, the Evans family finds itself under siege; the children's mild squabbles pale into insignificance beside the constant beating the whole family takes from the outside world, the perilous city that begins to appear with some frequency in later episodes of Lear's series. The anxiety about sheer survival intensifies with the death of Florida's husband James, turning the Evanses into that resonant sociological category, the single-parent, female-headed household. In *Good Times* the "outside" is hostile and filled with trouble, compounded by a parade of dumb or insensitive public officials (even the janitor is against them), and the family is squeezed inward, thrown back on itself for survival.

Family solidarity and obligation are central themes in *The Jeffersons* and *Sanford and Son* too. What has changed is that there is no longer a consensus about what these concepts mean, particularly between parents and children but also, increasingly, between spouses. The Sanfords, father and son, are always arguing about the ethics of means and ends. Lamont is forever trying to escape his background, improve himself, and, in the meantime, polish up his cheerfully decrepit father and render him more presentable. *Sanford and Son* offers a pale version of the British sitcom that inspired it. *Steptoe and Son* derives its eccentric force from the layers upon layers of hostility, mistrust, and emotional manipulation that masked the final, grudging allegiance of father and son. Lear sentimentalizes the relationship to fit the more equivocal sensibility of American network television.

The Jeffersons, like *All in the Family,* offers us domestic mayhem, a perpetual cycle of quarreling and reconciliation from which the dramatis personae never emerge. This is a family without a history and without development or resolution. Its characters are trapped in the recurring angry exchanges of stand-up comedy. George and Louise clash about what counts as ethical behavior. George and Lionel argue about race and politics. George drowns Tom and Helen in an endless barrage of insults about their mixed marriage. With Florence the maid he is immersed in a full-scale war, just as he is with the world at large. Only toward his mother, a whiny, self-absorbed hypochondriac whom everyone else loathes, does George, Oedipus forever unresolved, show an uncritical deference. As with the Bunkers, the Jefferson household serves as a stage on which major points of social tension are mounted as abstract "issues" and fought over in an eternal, conflicted status quo in which each new episode can proceed as though its past never existed. In Lear's shows the capacity of comedy to subvert or challenge received ideas sometimes stops short at noisy catharsis. Blacks and other minorities may, as Edith Bunker ingenuously puts it, have "come a long way on TV," but neither blacks nor whites know how to make sense of the changes in their lives. The focus on ethnic conflict in Lear's shows, so resonant in the wider culture during this period, threatens to become dissipated, first, by its immersion in the private discourse of family and, second, by the woolly, unspecific brand of humanism that marks the discourse of television when it seeks the middle ground of the mass audience while holding onto the more lucrative demographic categories.

In Chapter 1 I argued that the gathering strength and influence of the women's movement in the late 1960s and early 1970s called attention to the critical position women had come to occupy at the intersection of family and workplace since World War II. As women entered the labor force and shouldered the multiple burdens of running domestic lives while fitting themselves into workplace cultures designed for men, the feminist critique of patriarchy in the private sphere as well as in the workplace became part of the fabric of public discussion. It also became part of the fabric of television "relevance." Because of its location in the home and its base in consumer advertising, network television has always been woman-oriented. In 1970 the adoption of "demographic" ratings strategies focused the attention of advertisers and programmers on urban women between the ages of eighteen and thirty-five as a top spending group, and this served to legitimize "women's issues" as a "relevant" topic in television series. At the same time the gains of the women's movement were being realized in a slow but significant increase in the hiring of women for positions in television production. Serafina Bathrick (1984) notes that 50 percent of the scripts accepted for *The Mary Tyler Moore Show* were written by women, and eight women won Emmy Awards for television production in 1974. Though far from typical of industry trends as a whole, this advance marked the beginning of a steady growth in women's involvement in television production that continued in the 1980s.

Out of this conjuncture of social and industrial changes emerged a "prime-time feminism" thoroughly in accordance with the commercial priorities of the networks. Though gender relations had always been implicit in television discourse, now they were integrated as explicit issues in top-rated shows. During the 1970s female characters grew more numerous in every genre. The majority of "women's series" (shows that revolved around women even though they were aimed at wider audiences) were comedies made by Norman Lear's Tandem Productions (*Maude* [1972], *Mary Hartman, Mary Hartman* [1975], *One Day at a Time* [1975]) and by MTM Productions (*The Mary Tyler Moore Show* [1970], *Rhoda* [1974]), which was headed in the 1970s by Grant Tinker and his then-wife Mary Tyler Moore. As a group these shows acknowledge significant changes in family structure and relationships more directly than others, giving a more powerful sense of the provisional nature of family ties than is apparent in the ethnic comedies.

The single women of television in the 1950s and 1960s had been either widows (*The Lucy Show*), husband-hungry spinsters (*Our Miss Brooks*), plain and therefore unmarriageable career women (Sally in *The Dick Van Dyke Show*), or temporarily unmarried with a faithful fiancé in tow (*That Girl*). They were either idiosyncratic exceptions to, or strays soon to be integrated into, a benign and

inviolate nuclear family. By contrast, the families of television
women in the 1970s are either troubled or have fallen apart
altogether. Typically these women are divorced or separated,
single parents, or single but decidedly unspinsterish career women.
The only full-time homemaker, Lear's Mary Hartman, inhabits a
collapsed domestic world, with her marriage, her immediate and
extended family, and eventually her mental health in total disarray.

Maude spun off Edith Bunker's opinionated, independent cousin
into her own series, which quickly found its way into the top ten and
remained popular until its final season in 1978, after which it
achieved some success in syndication. A wealthy, middle-aged New
York suburbanite, Maude is a progovernment liberal and an
outspoken feminist, familiar to viewers through her verbal duels
with Archie, from which she usually emerged victorious. Like
Archie, Maude has loudly voiced opinions on every subject and,
like him too, she is generally angry on principle. There is the same
parade of topical debates, running from welfare liberalism to
free-enterprise conservatism, and the same gradual transition from
wider policy issues to more diffuse "family" problems. Maude's
strident confidence in the essential correctness of her world view is
tempered or silenced by the intractability or complexity of, variously, her husband Walter's alcoholism and bankruptcy, his nervous breakdown, her own pregnancy in middle age, and her de-
cision to have an abortion. Aside from her political activism, Maude
regularly confronts the predictable crises of aging such as menopause or whether to have a face-lift, and as time goes on, the social
issues take a back seat to more private concerns, as they did in *All
in the Family*.

The show is full of marriage and remarriage, equally full of
marital discord, disruption, and renewal. Walter is Maude's fourth
husband (she has been divorced three times). Her daughter Carol,
also divorced, lives with Maude and Walter together with her son
Philip; she has many affairs and comes close to remarrying, but the
wedding is called off and the prospective husband disappears from
the series. Maude's best friend Vivian, also divorced, marries
Maude's next door neighbor. It is as if the family had been swept
into a perpetual state of dissolution and recombination, an effect
reinforced by the spinoff device itself, which shunts the viewer from
one seething, provisional union to the next.

The single parent has always been a powerful image in television entertainment. In the 1950s and 1960s it was almost invariably couched in widowhood, though there were often hints of divorce, usually visited on supporting or morally ambiguous characters.[6] In the shows of the early 1970s divorce and separation move closer to the surface, helped by the ensemble casts, in which subordinate regular characters could bear the weight of marital collapse, leaving central ones uncontaminated. But producers still circled warily around divorce for central characters in domestic series. Though Edith Bunker has a plentiful supply of relatives, usually women, in varying states of marital disorder, her own marriage remains solid (if much discussed), as does that of George and Louise Jefferson. Maude, though divorced several times, now enjoys a lasting marriage. *One Day at a Time*, Norman Lear's last comedy to sustain a presence in the top ten, is the first series to focus on the character and concerns of a divorcée.

The series begins in 1975 with Ann Romano, a thirty-five-year-old "displaced homemaker," picking up the pieces of a seventeen-year marriage she had devoted to caring for her husband and her two daughters, Julie and Barbara, now in their teens. Ann's picture-book nuclear family has dissolved before her eyes, taking with it the well-trodden routines of her roles as wife and mother, and now she must grow up all over again under vastly different conditions. The show is not only about Ann but also about the new family she fashions, gathering together the unraveled threads of other attachments and other families. In addition to her daughters, there is Dwayne Schneider, the blustery janitor who wanders in and out of Ann's apartment at will, getting in the way and dispensing gratuitous and largely faulty advice but rapidly finding a place in the hearts of the Romano women. Schneider takes his place in a long line of castrated males in television entertainment, men who make themselves absurd with tough macho talk, who are safe because they have been stripped of the sexual challenge that complicates relations between men and women, and who melt into vulnerability and loving support when the chips are down.

Later in the series Ann's father dies and her widowed mother becomes an eccentric addition to the family. The two women dance loving but wary circles around each other, battling over territory, knowledge, and rules. Still later a new offspring is drafted into this innovative family in the person of Alex, a teenager from a problem family in Chicago. When a visiting Soviet basketball team asks to see a typical American family, Ann extends her hospitality, drawing from her precocious foster son the dry comment: "Hey, we're a typical American family—a divorced mother of two, a twenty-year-old daughter who still lives at home, and a displaced teenager from Chicago!"

The vital center of this motley crew is Ann herself, facing a whole new range of tasks and roles—she must find work, learn to discipline as well as nurture, and carve out a fresh identity for herself as a woman. Ann is negotiating uncharted normative territory; she is forced to invent her own rules for living. Of her fifteen-year-old daughter she remarks ruefully, "I didn't get to be her age until I was thirty-four!" In these "women's comedies" there is little of the hot debating of formalized political agendas, war, corrupt government, or industrial pollution that punctuate Lear's earlier comedies. Ann Romano contends with different problems, apparently closer to home. Her father infantilizes her; her mother interferes or competes; her daughters run away with boyfriends. Can she trust a newly qualified doctor to operate on her daughter's appendix? Will her daughters repeat her marital mistakes? What has she achieved? Is it all downhill from here?

Where Archie, George, and even Maude confront the world as a configuration of abstract institutions and rush at life's obstacles with blazing rhetoric and dogmatic bravado, Ann Romano typically engages in a holding action, weathering specific situations one by one. "Just hold on tight, we'll muddle through / One day at a time," the title song reminds her, and us, each week. Mass-market series, as I have shown, must tend toward the affirmative and redemptive, and so they continue to tend with Ann and other television heroines of the period. Yet now the genre's "think positive" sensibility is tinged with desperation. To be heroic one is no longer required to win, merely to survive, and to bounce back fighting, or at least coping.

Of course Ann does win, in ways that elude many of the women, particularly the single mothers, who watch her show. She gets a job as an accounts executive in an advertising agency and goes into partnership with her friend Francine (depicted as a less principled, manipulative career woman with few personal ties). Ann dates frequently; her daughters both marry good men. But these achievements, no doubt realizing vicariously the dreams of many women viewers, are not the show's central concerns, which focus on the parade of largely domestic crises that plague Ann's weekly life and, beyond them, questions of her own developing identity as an independent woman. Ann resumes her maiden name, correcting others who address her as Mrs. instead of Ms. She will not allow others, particularly male others, to tell her what to do.

Like other shows centering on women's lives, *One Day at a Time* is primarily concerned with social learning, with problems of individual and family identity, parenting, and authority in a world where women who would otherwise remain untouched by feminism are forced by circumstances to contemplate independence and come to cherish it. This "populist feminism" may be one reason for the show's longevity (it continued until June 1984); unlike Gloria Bunker, who seems to pull her feminism out of a textbook, Ann discovers the energies of the women's movement organically, through the experience of standing alone in a man's world. Another reason may be that the show hedges its bets in its portrayal of women, satisfying a wide range of male and female ideals. Ann herself is spunky, capable yet insecure, attractive yet ordinary-looking. Her mother provides the combination of frontierswoman bluntness and idiosyncratic nuttiness so often found in television renditions of older American women. Julie, her elder daughter, is the quintessential wild adolescent. Barbara is the good girl, the sweet thing, who, in her mother's words, "happens to have been born wise"; and she marries that emblem of steady respectability, a dentist. In this ensemble there is something for everybody, allowing the viewer to identify with the "new woman" while hanging on to older ideals of femininity—and retaining for the show its male audience.

Ann learns to be an adult, a new woman, and a new kind of parent. If feminism helps her to redefine the terms of her life, so too does a highly contemporary psychological sensibility, which comes to usurp the language of ethics as a basis for action. An episode in which Ann's father pays the Romanos a visit is illustrative. His arrival coincides with yet another crisis: Barbara is missing, along with her boyfriend. Mr. Romano, an exhausted-looking Italian-American, immediately muscles in, trying to recreate the unquestioned authority he has enjoyed for so long in his own home. He disapproves of Ann's divorce from the husband he found for her: "For eighteen generations the Romanos have never had a divorce . . . your cousin Rosalie, she got a Ph. D. You, you got a divorce!" He tries to persuade her to move back home. He frowns on her daughters' wardrobes and their boyfriends and disapproves of Ann's laissez-faire style of childrearing. He is by turns meddling, furious, and overprotective. Ann resists firmly, issue by issue, but soon the argument broadens into a more general conflict about autonomy and generational change, couched in the insights of the psychology of self-actualization:

> *Ann:* Dad, these are my children! And yes, we have troubles, and yes, they make mistakes, and it is tough without a man— tough on them and tough on me . . . everybody's always trying to make things easy for me . . . I had a domineering husband, I have a domineering father . . . I'm thirty-five years old, and I'm pleading with my father . . . good lord, it's a programmed response!

> *Father:* You sound like you been going to one of them shrinks [that] teach the children to hate their parents!

> *Ann:* I don't hate my parents, I'm just doing what I want to do. You make it sound like a due bill . . . we gave you love and braces, now give *us* something!

> *Father:* Don't children have any feelings toward their parents any more?

> *Ann:* Yes, you've got my love. But my life, that's mine! . . . you wrapped us all in this protective cocoon, but that's not the way the world is. No more, dad, not for me . . . and if I can find the strength, not for Julie and Barbara. Can you understand that?

> *Father:* Yes . . . no . . . I'm trying to understand . . . the world is all different today . . . I miss knowing that you're in the same city, a couple of blocks away. Since you went away my life has been kind of empty.

Another episode replicates this conflict and its narrative progression almost to the letter. This time, however, it is Julie who has run away with her boyfriend. As Ann's rage and anxiety spill over onto her other daughter, their exchange echoes the gap

between the generations, the bewilderment about the proper way
to set an example for one's children, that took place between Ann
and her father:

> *Ann:*   I don't think this whole thing would've happened without
> the divorce . . . I'm the one who's always talking about
> *finding* myself, leading an independent life . . . why the
> hell *should* Julie act any differently?

Unsure how to act, she vacillates:

> *Ann:*   I'm calling the police . . . I don't know what else to do
> but sit here and wait . . . I feel so helpless! . . . oh,
> Barbara, it's all so frustrating! You live your life, you make
> mistakes, you try to learn from them. When you try to pass
> on that knowledge to your kids, they not only don't learn,
> they resent you for it.
>
> *Barbara:*   . . . It's frustrating for kids too! First you say grow up,
> make your own decisions, then when we do, you say, what
> did you do that for?

For Ann and her father, indeed for "the girls" too, the rules for
living have been thrown out of joint. Caught in the tension between
authority (implying security as well as repression) and freedom
(implying confusion as well as independence), they are plunged into
an ambiguous set of realities that compel them to invent themselves
as they go along, "one day at a time." But there are limits. When
Ann and Julie finally confront one another, and Julie presents her
mother with a list of demands that includes the abolition of all rules,
the boundaries of permissiveness become clear. Ann digs her heels
in, telling her daughter she need not bother to come home on those
terms—and earning a vigorous round of applause from the audience
for her assertion of authority. This is the television narrative having
it both ways, avoiding divisive issues that might split the audience
by endorsing both tradition and modernity, freedom and restraint,
by raising an intractable problem and then solving it.

If the women's comedy confronts head-on the inadequacy of
traditional family norms, it also expresses, sometimes painfully, a
profound confusion about the boundaries that divide private from
public authority. The language of *One Day at a Time* reflects a
formal respect for professionals, particularly those whose skills and
authority overlap with (or usurp) those of parents, yet it also betrays

a deep mistrust. Ann is a thoroughly modern parent, versed in
received therapeutic wisdom. When Schneider's visiting adolescent nephew enrages his uncle by cheating, lying, and compul-
sively stealing, Ann chides him: "Did you ever stop to think for a
second that he might *want* to get caught? People do all kinds of
crazy things to get attention. Maybe he needs professional help, a
psychiatrist." But when the prospect of professional help comes
closer to home, she is less receptive. Julie comes down with
appendicitis, and Ann has a hard time finding an available and, in
her demanding eyes, suitably skilled physician. The family
discussion abounds with resentment of the medical profession: "I'm
going to call Dr. Redman. He can't be playing golf this time of
night"; "I don't have a doctor. Doctors make me sick"; "Doctors are
never there when you want one"; "Be nice to this one, 'cause today's
doctors are tomorrow's landlords. They got condominiums, they
got everything." And when Ann expresses her doubts about the
competence of a young, casually dressed intern at the hospital, the
joke becomes the parroted response she gets, over and over again,
from the staff: "If he's on the staff, he's got to be good." Frustrated,
she asks an older doctor, "How do you find out if a doctor's good, if
you're all trying to protect each other?" and when he parries with a
standard piece of public relations, "We're trying to maintain a high
standard of medicine, and thereby protect the patient," she
counters sharply, "That's a crock!"

Following *All in the Family*, Lear's ethnic comedies had returned
the television sitcom to its earlier form—a string of jokes draped
over thin plots and characters, but now infused with the deadly
serious aggression only comedy, perhaps, can offer in a medium as
closely scrutinized for physical violence as is television. This format
left little room for the development of character and relationship, so
that family was little more than a seething forum for rage contained
within formalized positions concerning race, gender, and class.
With *One Day at a Time* the domestic comedy evolves into the
more flexible form of what Jane Feuer (1984) calls the "character
comedy," with the jokes interspersed with straight drama and
integrated into a family chronicle. The stories repeat themselves,
but characters develop and acquire new knowledge about the
world, and we about them. The story of Julie's break for freedom is
carried over three episodes. Thus the expanded narrative becomes

the occasion for a protracted meditation on divorce, parenting, and the generation gap. Julie's capitulation and voluntary return to the bosom of her family suggest that home is best even when its norms and its boundaries are inadequate and provisional. But this form also signifies, as did *All in the Family*, the genre straining at its own boundaries. Comedy takes a back seat to dramatic dialogue, and action is accomplished through, or eclipsed by, talk. Indeed, *One Day at a Time* often approaches the serial conventions of the soap opera, with its endless stream of personal crises dissolving rather than resolving, its heavy psychological overtones, its preoccupation with "women's" concerns, and its emphasis on relationship rather than event. It may be that the soap opera, reflecting institutionalized flux and unresolved crisis, serves as a more resonant modernist form than the series, as is evident from the flourishing daytime soaps and the proliferation of nighttime soaps in the 1980s.

In fact Tandem's next offering, aired in January 1976, was *Mary Hartman, Mary Hartman*, which self-consciously transcended the boundaries of the episodic series by offering a parody of the daytime soap opera. Because of its innovative form (it was designed for daily half-hour showings) and its frank rather than prurient attention to sex, the show was rejected by all three networks, including CBS, which had financed the pilot. Lear, who was convinced he had created a potential hit, was able to mobilize his substantial capital resources and his reputation as the top producer of the decade to sell the show directly to fifty-four local stations, in effect creating his own syndicate. Placed in a late-night time slot, the show not only gathered a cult following but became a national hit, outstripping even the late-night local news shows in the ratings. Despite its success with audiences, however, *Mary Hartman, Mary Hartman* was losing money because of its low trial sponsorship fee. By the time companies like Metromedia were ready to offer higher rates, the strain of producing five episodes a week was taking its toll, and at the end of the second season the show's star, Louise Lasser, announced she was leaving. In the rationalized world in which television genres grow, radical departures from standard form and presentation find it difficult to survive.

One of the most arresting innovations in television's copycat history, *Mary Hartman, Mary Hartman* showed a capacity during its relatively short life for leaping from one set of genre conventions to another, from comedy to satire to drama, from serial to series. Produced in half-hour segments like the episodic series, it nonetheless approaches the soap opera format, with a large cast, meandering, open-ended plots, and plenty of breathy melodrama. It begins as a comedy, but the laughter grows more and more painful. In early episodes *Mary Hartman* adheres closely to the rules of parody—exaggeration and contrast. The show chronicles the interwoven lives of three crisis-ridden families in the small, unglamorous company town of Fernwood, Ohio. Soapier than any bona fide soap, though, all three families fairly shriek with catastrophe. They are plagued with external threats (a mass murderer stalks the town and takes Mary hostage; the neighborhood flasher is revealed as her beloved grandfather; husband Tom's job at the plant is beset with industrial strife and the permanent specter of unemployment) but these families are also unraveling at the seams. Mary, the lethargic but anxious homemaker at the show's center, is trying to save her troubled marriage. Tom has become impotent; her sister Cathy seeks love through a series of wildly inappropriate affairs; her daughter Heather is always preparing to run away. Mary herself is poised, week after week, on the brink of an affair with a seductive local policeman.

Although the tone of *Mary Hartman* sounds like a soap opera spinning out of control, its visual cues have none of the glamor of that form. The sets, with their drab kitchens and kitschy living rooms decorated straight from mail-order catalogues and department store shelves, are overstated icons of modern working-class life. Mary is no soap opera heroine, indeed no television heroine of any kind to date, with her pigtails and girlish calico dresses. James Monaco (1981) has noted the similarity between Mary's getup and that of another media Mary, "little" Mary Pickford. The difference is that the earlier Mary was ingenuously complemented by her surroundings and by the narrative, whereas Mary Hartman's retarded personal style stands in ludicrous contrast to her environment and its themes, with her soulful voice droning on and her glassy-eyed obsession with the "waxy yellow buildup" on the kitchen floor. Her daughter Heather, an embodiment of the gawky teenager, peers myopically at the world through tortoise-shell glasses and slouches sullenly around the house. Her mother, inverting the dominant, well-groomed matriarch so seminal to the soap opera, hovers about wispily with furrowed brow, wringing her hands ineffectually and offering breezily inappropriate aphorisms. Her friend Loretta Haggers aspires to country-and-western stardom while embracing fundamentalist religion; and Loretta's husband Charlie's reputed sexual prowess contrasts oddly with his workaday looks and dilapidated attire.

Over time, parody slides uneasily in and out of melodrama. Cues for audience laughter grow fuzzier. Other shows, in the early 1970s, juxtapose comedy and drama, but the boundaries remain relatively clear. In *Mary Hartman* what is funniest is also most devastating, and the humor is offset by an undertone of violence: Mary's neighbor drowns in a bowl of chicken soup she has brought over to speed his recovery from an illness; Jimmy Jo Jeeter, the child evangelist, is electrocuted in his bath; Mary's grandfather is arrested for flashing. Maude and Ann Romano may have their troubles, but Mary Hartman's world is disintegrating, and so, eventually, does Mary. The anxiety that gathered momentum in Lear's earlier comedies here seeps into every crevice of daily life, becoming ubiquitous and, finally, disabling. Not only is Mary's immediate external world full of threat and disaster; not only is her family falling apart. Mary is menaced also from within by a diffuse but paralyzing malaise she can neither understand nor overcome.

Locked inside her home by her housewife role, Mary is effectively sealed off from direct engagement with the outside world. She becomes a walking example of "media consciousness." Her major sources of information, advice, and reassurance are the media. From magazines and movies, and particularly from the television that sits permanently switched on in her kitchen, Mary struggles to assimilate an avalanche of images offering her consumer goods and cheap psychological homilies. Her deepening panic and depression are punctuated with staccato, disordered rushes of enthusiasm for each proffered solution—a new floor polish, the therapeutic cult STET (a thinly disguised jibe at EST) pushed on her by Sergeant Foley and her grandfather's social worker, the fundamentalist folk wisdom that sustains her friend Loretta—and as each fails to stem the tide of her despair, she slumps, disillusioned, back into her ennui. *Mary Hartman* provides the sharpest and most sustained critique of television, psychology, and media-fed knowledge in general to date. Its attack on consumerism is lent grotesque force by the commercials that break up the show; Mary's war against "waxy yellow buildup" is ranged alongside advertisements for products that create it or fight it. And when she is chosen to appear on *The David Susskind Show* as the "Number One Typical American Housewife," she succumbs, a true victim of the feminine mystique, to an on-screen nervous collapse.

Life gets worse. Mary begins her second season as a patient at the Fernwood mental hospital, which has been designated one of the "average TV households" selected by the Nielsen company to measure national viewing habits.[7] Back home she and Tom struggle to rise above the chaos of their private lives, only to find themselves negotiating a world populated by opportunists and tricksters: the smooth-talking Sergeant Foley, the evangelist Merle Jeeter peddling his own little boy as a healer, the conman who takes over the management of Loretta's singing career from her husband and cheats them of their royalties. Finally, Mary runs away with Sergeant Foley, only to replicate the conditions of her former life.

And yet, full as it is of disaster, loss, and pain, *Mary Hartman* is also full of dissent, of people fighting back and trying to transcend the stifling conditions under which they live. Loretta wants to be a star; her husband wants only to help make her one. Tom wants a decent, secure job and an honest union. Cathy, for all her sexual carelessness, is looking for a permanent partner. Tom and Mary try repeatedly to gather the fraying ends of their marriage and make it work. Even Mary, who does not know what is wrong or what would put it right, knows something is wrong and struggles to resolve it. Her problem is that she can choose only from the range of shoddy cultural options her life offers her—television, consumer goods, and pop psychology.

As Barbara Ehrenreich (1976) has pointed out, alongside the fragmentation and the dissolution are powerful images of kindness, community, and solidarity, of people bewilderedly trying to do right by each other. Mary and Loretta sustain and encourage one another. Despite their competition for the attentions of Sergeant Foley, Mary tries to protect her sister Cathy from harm. Tom, Charlie, and George Shumway are workmates and friends, loyal to each other despite the difficulty they have in communicating their affection. *Mary Hartman* comes closer than any other Lear show, perhaps closer than any other television series, to uncovering both the "hidden injuries" and the resilience of a damaged working-class culture still bound together, at least in the discourse of television, by the energy and mutual loyalty of its women.

The family comedies of Norman Lear dominated the Nielsen top ten for the first half of the 1970s and continued to make their mark throughout the decade, although they were displaced from the top positions in mid-decade by the new hits from ABC. The only other production company that achieved substantial ratings and critical success during this period and developed a distinctive "house style" was Grant Tinker's MTM Productions. MTM's was a quieter "relevance" with more verbal comedy, in which social issues emerged, as one of the chief writers observed, out of the quotidian problems of "people just trying to get through the day." The strength of the company lay in innovative shows set in workplaces rather than in homes—comedies such as *The Mary Tyler Moore Show*, *WKRP in Cincinnati*, and *The Bob Newhart Show* and, later, dramatic series such as *Lou Grant* and *Hill Street Blues*.

MTM's only successful domestic comedy was *Rhoda*, a spin-off from *The Mary Tyler Moore Show* that moved Mary's acerbic, lively neighbor back to her native city of New York. The series ran for four years (two in the top twenty) and continued to flourish for a while in the 1980s in syndication. Witty, flamboyant in dress and speech, the perfect foil for Mary's wholesome small-town respectability, Rhoda Morgenstern is also conspicuously Jewish. Like the Lear series, MTM comedies are infused with the proud secular ethnicity that has come to define the episodic series in the 1980s. *Rhoda* is also aimed at women audiences and speaks to contemporary women's issues, though in a far less strident voice than the Lear comedies. Rhoda's main project in life in *The Mary Tyler Moore Show* had been a cheerful but fruitless search for a husband. In the first episode of her own series she meets and falls in love with Joe Gerard, a handsome young divorced man with one son (who lives with his mother) and all the right credentials; he is Jewish, good-looking, amiable, and a successful partner in the ominously named New York Wrecking Company. A sixty-minute special is soon devoted to Rhoda and Joe's wedding, complete with her old buddies from *The Mary Tyler Moore Show*, capturing record ratings for CBS.

But if all the world loves a television wedding, it is less

enthusiastic about a marriage. Critics complained that life with
Rhoda and Joe was dull and lacked dramatic tension. Certainly
during this period the narrative relies on Rhoda's besetting
insecurities. Her "lifelong terror of beautiful blondes" erupts when
she meets Joe's attractive ex-wife and when her sister Brenda's
roommate makes eyes at Joe, which he receives with a smiling
equanimity bordering on inanity. In 1976 the show's creators
responded to criticism by having Rhoda and Joe separate. As is
common in Lear's series, episodes are strung together like a kind of
miniseries under a single theme, not so much to advance a "plot" as
to explore the development of character and relationships in
conflict. Here comedy and painful drama mingle as the sequence of
episodes entitled "Rhoda's Marital Mishaps" rehearses in graphic
detail her strenuous efforts to save the marriage without compro-
mising her conditions for its integrity. Joe moves out of their
Manhattan apartment and the couple begins "dating," an arrangement that suits him perfectly and her not at all. Rhoda drags her
reluctant spouse to a marriage counselor, and subsequent scenes
combine a wicked commentary on psychotherapeutic jargon and
technique with a skillful evocation of the widening gap between
male and female perceptions of marriage. Joe is quite content to go
on dating; he loves his wife but sees no reason to be married: "I'm
not sure that I wanna be married. If I wanna be married you're as
good as I can get . . . you *made* me marry you!"

Significantly, *Rhoda*'s ratings dropped during this period. Either
the critics were wrong or perhaps the tension and suffering had
gone from too little to too much. The process of separation and
Rhoda's recovery is finely—possibly too finely—observed; Rhoda
alternately humiliates herself by running after her husband and
achieves a precarious dignity by getting on with her own life. But
for a while the show is all tragic soap opera and no transcendence.
In *The Mary Tyler Moore Show* Mary, the malleable, accommodating girl next door, and Rhoda, the brash, self-deprecating,
overweight New Yorker, had matured and grown sophisticated
together—each wanting a man, neither desperate for one, and
satisfied in each other's company. Here is Rhoda grown desperate
again, and it may have been that audiences (particularly women)
were unwilling to contemplate their heroine prostrate with grief,
preferring what they had seen in Mary Richards and Ann Romano:

a woman on her own, facing obstacles but weathering them with strength and composure.

In 1977 this was exactly what they got; in any event the ratings rose again. Rhoda is reestablished as a single working woman, suffering with her sister Brenda (who now assumes Rhoda's earlier role, charming and droll put plump and insecure) the anxieties and disappointments of dating but poised and confident, absorbed in her work first as a window dresser, then as a costume maker. She is at once ordinary (subject to failure and rejection) and glamorous (she is creative and dresses with Bohemian panache). Men can irritate and upset her, but the viewer is given the sense that there is little Rhoda could not survive, echoing Ann Romano's sturdy durability in *One Day at a Time*. Rhoda regains control of her life as the focus of the show shifts to the workplace, where she goes into business for herself.

For all their differences in tone and setting, the similarities between *Rhoda* and other women-oriented shows are striking. All are about women learning to live without men. The men are either absent (Ann Romano's ex-husband), weak and childish (Ted Baxter in *The Mary Tyler Moore Show*), insubstantial (Rhoda's husband Joe), asexual (Murray Slaughter in *The Mary Tyler Moore Show*, Dwayne Schneider in *One Day at a Time*) or fatherly (Lou Grant in *The Mary Tyler Moore Show*) and therefore taboo. Rhoda's and Brenda's apartments become home territory to a procession of inadequate, if likable, men (Benny, Gary, the cabaret singer Johnny Venture, and of course the invisible inebriate "Carlton-your-doorman"). The women gather around themselves a provisional domesticity with ad hoc families, whether related by blood or not. They would like to be married but are far from desperate, and their emotional nourishment comes from one another—friends, sisters, mothers, and daughters. Rhoda and Brenda wander freely between separate apartments in the same building. They unite frequently in an affectionate power struggle with their mother Ida, a manipulative but lovable matriarch who finds her daughters' lives incomprehensible, not at all what she had in mind for them. Rhoda's father is a warm but passive figure who eventually disappears to Florida to "find himself," leaving Ida free to become a dissenting participant in the "women's culture" her daughters have propagated.

Once again the viewer is invited to contemplate the confusion of family and marriage. In part it is a battle of the sexes; Rhoda and Joe have different ideas about what counts as marriage and, for that matter, separation. In sporadic efforts to be modern, Ida declares her wish to be her daughters' friend, a wish that falls on deaf ears since, for all the friction, what "the girls" want is a mother. In one episode the yawning gap between generations is illustrated when Gary Levy (one of Brenda's platonic, loser companions) is pressured by his parents to bring home the steady girlfriend he does not have but has constructed over the years in an elaborate fiction to quiet their demands that he settle down. He drags an unwilling Rhoda instead, and the web of lies they must improvise to shore up the initial deception collapses when Gary's mother notices Rhoda's wedding ring. In despair at life's unremitting barrage of unpleasant surprises, Rhoda confides to Brenda her favorite fantasy, in which she gathers everyone she ever knew in Yankee Stadium and tells them, "All right, everybody, start apologizing!" Like many other sitcoms of the period, *Rhoda* becomes less a succession of plots built around the resolution of situational asymmetry than a chronicle of lives lived in new kinds of primary grouping. In these new sitcoms people make up rules and roles as they negotiate the common hurts of their time, and transcend them, if only by cheerful survival.

The "women's comedy" takes the evolution of the sitcom further along the path to character comedy than any other television form. What happens serves less to push along and tie up events than to foster viewer attachment to an ensemble of characters and to cement their relationships. The plots, such as they are, are about women negotiating uncharted normative territory because they are single, or single again, or because they work in a man's world. The rules for guidance on which they were raised are inadequate, inappropriate, or simply not there when it comes to dating after thirty, raising children without a man, or establishing respect and authority in the workplace. These women are plunged, week after week, into an ambiguous world that compels them to reinvent themselves as they go along.

By the mid-1970s feminism is thoroughly integrated into the liberal discourse of television entertainment, especially in shows that center on women; but in some series it suffers from the same problems that have beset some explicitly feminist fiction. At its most self-conscious and didactic (as in the early Lear shows), prime-time feminism can be wooden and speechy, an abstract ideology carefully injected into characters that become representational stick figures. It works best when it flows (half-consciously, perhaps, in producers' minds) through the lives of women forced by disturbing changes in their marital and family arrangements to reassess the assumptions that guide their lives—Ann Romano alone with two children at age thirty-five; Rhoda alone *again* in her mid-thirties; Brenda struggling with her weight, her insecurities, and her dependent boyfriends; Ida Morgenstern trying to comprehend the puzzling conditions that push and pull at her daughters' lives. Some of the most striking unspoken commentary on postwar attitudes about women's roles emerges in *Mary Hartman*, in the absurd contrasts between the cultural legacy that makes Mary dress like a child of ten and the monumentally grown-up problems she faces as her marriage and family collapse about her. These prime-time feminists are ordinary women whose lives would otherwise remain untouched by the women's movement but who are forced by circumstance to contemplate independence and come to champion it for its own sake.

Chapter 5 takes up these themes as they affect television women in the workplace, and I shall show that the "women's comedy," in common with other forms of "feminine narrative," pulls its audience in different directions.[5] By positing a consistent imagery of cooperation and solidarity among capable, autonomous women, television comedy opens both a space for the expression of dissatisfaction with existing gender roles and a vision of community that suggests alternatives to the nuclear family. At the same time these alternatives are tamed and contained by the reconciliation of awkward contradictions and role conflicts that beset women in everyday life at home and at work.

For most of the 1970s the half-hour comedy monopolized both the top twenty in the ratings and the domestic sphere, while the hour-long drama became the preserve of action-adventure series. Only three dramatic series set in the home became ratings hits in the 1970s: *The Waltons* (1972), *Little House on the Prairie* (1974), and *Family* (1976). A weekly series about a rural family in Depression-era Appalachia, *The Waltons* seems an odd choice for a network bent on shedding its older viewers for more youthful, urban constituencies. But like its generic ancestor *Bonanza*, *The Waltons* inserts a distinctly modern sensibility into a rural past lavishly upholstered in nostalgia. Narrated by the eldest son, John-Boy (an aspiring novelist with the hurt, angelic face of a country innocent), the series chronicles the weekly doings of a three-generation, white Baptist family—grandparents, parents, and seven children—through the Depression, the Second World War, and the accelerated change of the postwar era. Significantly, it aired in a period when viewers were weathering Vietnam, Watergate, and economic recession. In a viewer's world beset by rapid, bewildering, and remote changes, Walton's Mountain offered the comforting culture of the local and the continuities of a perfect gemeinschaft—a harmonious, solidary family embedded in a tiny, organic community padded out with two elderly spinsters and the childless couple that runs the village store.

The Waltons is a conventional episodic drama, combining repetition (the weekly happy ending, in which a member of the family has learned an experiential lesson in love or ethics to tuck away for future use) with the continuity of a regular ensemble of characters whose development viewers can follow season by season. Without the conflict and aggression that comedy can safely harbor, *The Waltons* turns populist sentimentality and earnest didacticism into a fine art. Each week a lesson in interpersonal relations or adaptation to inevitable change is internalized by one or another member of the family. John-Boy, accompanying an old lady to the seashore where all her memories lie or delivering the baby of a young Appalachian mother, learns that the raw material for his writing lies in the everyday experience of ordinary folks. His mother Olivia discovers that her fit of restlessness with domesticity and her desire to pursue her musical talents are but passing fads—the family is all she really needs for fulfillment. His sister Erin falls in love with a spoiled rich boy who is at odds with his domineering father, teaches him the ethics of family solidarity and open communication, and draws her own lessons about love along the way.

Most often the learning relies on a developmental model of maturation that requires accommodation to change, whether within the family itself or in the world outside. But if the setting is solemnly rustic and "historical," the tone is decidedly modern, with moral categories increasingly being redefined in psychological language. Elizabeth, the youngest of the seven children, is growing into adolescence, and she misses her absent parents and feels rejected by her siblings, who are all busy with their own projects. "You don't understand!" she cries to her brother Jason, "When you were growing up, you had Mama and Daddy, and Grandma and Grandpa too . . . but I don't . . . it's different for me!" "I'm only your brother," pleads Jason, very much the contemporary adolescent for all his flannel-shirted, overalled rural simplicity. "I don't know how to be anybody else . . . you expect us to fill the void in your life . . . we all love you, but we can't do that." And Rose, the nurturant matron filling in for Elizabeth's parents, tells her, "That's the way families are, Elizabeth. They grow up and they grow away." The closing voice-over drives the message home: "It was a time of discovery for the family . . . that it is possible to choose relatives as friends. [They] found out that the family fabric gave from time to time, but the mending always made it stronger." This in reference to a period when it would have occurred to nobody to "choose relatives as friends."

This blend of tradition and modernity may account for the success of the series with sophisticated 1970s audiences. The Waltons are an imaginary, idealized family set in an imaginary, idealized past, equipped with the insights of applied psychology. They offer us a world in which traditional values of faith and kindness, persistence and initiative, respond to modern dilemmas of identity and development, and in which the aphoristic, material language of common sense mingles happily with contemporary psychological wisdom. In *The Waltons* not only children learn; development is a lifelong process. In later seasons the young teach their elders. "Don't people ever recover from nervous break-downs?" asks middle-aged Rose fearfully when her suitor Stanley Perkins confesses to a spell in a mental hospital after being fired from his thirty-seven-year job as a traveling salesman. "It takes time," Mary Ellen, a qualified nurse in her twenties, explains gently, "and a lot of little successes." But for all the therapeutic rhetoric, it is Rose and the Waltons who repair the hapless Stanley, drawing him back into the organic life of their community, demonstrating their confidence in his capacity to work creatively, even presenting him with the gold watch his firm had failed to provide. The harboring and healing of lost or damaged refugees from a cruel outside world is a constant theme in the series, making Walton's Mountain truly a haven in a heartless institutional world.

Often, too, the conflict set up in each weekly narrative has the up-to-date flavor of current social problems. A Native American lays claim to Walton's Mountain as an ancestral burying ground. Jason's fiancée Toni announces that she is Jewish and sets off a domestic crisis about anti-Semitism and the effects of intermarriage on the integrity of the family unit. Prospecting for gold with a Geiger counter, local storekeeper Ike Godsey stumbles on radioactive waste dumped by a nearby laboratory and carries out his civic duty by reporting it to the authorities, forcing them to take action. And in a moment of before-the-fact historical insight, his wife Cora-Beth (who is planning to go into real estate) announces proudly that she is "expecting a postwar boom any day now." Like many other television shows, *The Waltons* rewrites history, juggling ideas of past and present drawn from Rockwellian fantasies of the self-sufficient community facing down the Goliath of the world-out-there.

The ratings success of *The Waltons* prompted NBC to create *Little House on the Prairie*, a virtual clone, which inherits from the popular *Bonanza* its 1870s frontier setting as well as its star, Michael Landon, who had played Little Joe in the earlier show. Based on Laura Ingalls Wilder's series of *Little House* children's books, the series replicates the format of close-knit rural family and community resisting the destructive forces of the external world by its own inner resources, guided by the firm yet rational and gentle (and decidedly modern in its psychological slant) authority of the Ingalls parents.

Like *The Waltons* and *Little House on the Prairie*, *Family* tells a continuing story of domestic unity and redemption. But its contemporary setting and concerns generate new meanings of unity and, for that matter, of family. Doug and Kate Lawrence are a well-to-do middle-aged couple (Doug is a successful lawyer in private practice) living in a comfortable Southern California suburb with their three children. Nancy, the eldest and a divorced single parent and law student, occupies the guest house at the end of the Lawrences' backyard with her small son, Timmy. She is replaced there in due course by Willie, the middle child, who in his early twenties already has a past stuffed with "relevant" experience. A dreamy high-school dropout and aspiring writer, Willie's first great love, Salina, was an unwed mother. He was married to Lizzie, who was carried off after three months by one of the convenient terminal illnesses that free bereaved television spouses to venture again into the outside world. The youngest daughter, Buddy (played by Kristy McNichol, an icon of the suburban American kid), is a model of tomboyish California normality, suffering through the usual rites of passage of the postwar adolescent.

Like the Waltons and the Ingalls, the Lawrences receive quantities of troubled strangers into their midst and heal their wounds. Here the outsiders run the gamut of contemporary social problems, taking the series further in the direction of soap opera. In a single episode Willie tries to fill the void left by his wife's death by "adopting" an underprivileged black teenager, while Buddy copes with a childhood friend who has become a teenage alcoholic. In other stories Doug and Kate stand up to a bigoted school committee on behalf of Buddy's lesbian teacher, setting an example in pluralist tolerance for their bewildered daughter. Willie tries to make an honest woman of a warmhearted prostitute friend by hiring her as his secretary. Nancy revives a romance with an old flame from college, now a promising young intern, only to discover that he is a drug addict. And if the troubled individuals pass out of the narrative strengthened by the Lawrences' kind integrity, the family members too have learned lessons in acceptance and the value of cultural diversity.

In this family, as in the contemporary soap opera, the problems are "inside" as well as "outside." Even Doug and Kate must weather the predictable crises of middle age. Doug almost has an affair with an attractive younger colleague (he resists, unlike the father of Buddy's friend Audrey, whose tawdry dalliance and the pain it brings his wife and children occupy the subplot and become a regular theme in the show). Like Olivia Walton, Kate becomes temporarily disaffected from her homemaking role but sees the light when she assists at the birth of a reluctant young mother and shows her how rewarding motherhood can be; subsequently she returns to her chosen career of music. She suffers breast cancer. Doug's mother dies; he himself is temporarily blinded in a car accident, and he must deal with his father's remarriage to a former cabaret singer with a shady past.

Doug and Kate have an unshakable marriage; together with Buddy, they are the family's companionate core. Willie and Nancy are its least stable members, forever attaching and detaching themselves from new relationships, hovering on the brink of remarriage and veering away, unable to make decisions until they are shown the way. The Lawrence family is simultaneously traditional and modern; the backyard guest house symbolizes its prodigal elements, always received back into the main house. In the characteristically redemptive television narrative the troubled present of the 1970s (Willie and Nancy) is sandwiched between the solid, traditional past (Doug and Kate) and the hopeful, wholesome future (Buddy). This may be a major part of *Family*'s appeal: it raises current problems and simultaneously assuages them by providing a supportive framework within the sphere of the domestic.

For all its preoccupation with social problems, *Family*'s primary arena, like that of other family dramas and soaps, is the "private" realm of feeling rather than action or event. The series makes the developmental psychology nascent in *The Waltons* its very heart. The tone is set by Kate, a combination of soft, full-figured, nurturant earth mother and enlightened modern parent, who shares with her husband the task of fostering autonomy and self-esteem in her children. "She's still scrambling around trying to figure out who she's going to be," Kate explains about Buddy to her emotionally precocious friend Mara. When Nancy, barely six months divorced, returns to live at home but shows every sign of rushing thoughtlessly into a second marriage, Kate fires off an ambiguous mixture of maternal concern and detached insight that lends a curious distance to the mother-daughter relationship, perhaps familiar to viewers from psychologically aware middle-class families. "You might try taking some responsibility for your own existence as an adult in this family," she chides Nancy, who has lumbered her mother with numerous domestic chores. "I think you ought to give yourself time to learn to handle your independence . . . I resent your low opinion of yourself. I know you're being torn apart by feelings you don't understand. I can only be here." It is a supportive yet curiously cool perceptiveness. This family does not need a caring professional; it has fully internalized the therapeutic sensibility, the language impregnated with insight. And everyone can learn, not just the younger generation. As Kate explains to Buddy when the family is riddled with strife on Christmas Eve, "The rest of us [adults] let so much get in the way of our feelings for each other, we need a special day."

The celebration of individual difference is a theme repeated over and over in *Family*. Colorful eccentrics and minorities parade happily through the narrative, their idiosyncrasies encouraged by the broad-minded Lawrences. Buddy learns, from her parents and her experience of life, to think for herself, make her own decisions, and not be swayed by majority opinion among her peers at school. The Lawrences exercise a firm yet permissive authority over their children; they know when to hang on and when to let go. On his twenty-first birthday Willie is plunged into a crisis of identity and declares his intention of leaving home to broaden the field of his experience. Doug persuades him not to go; his creative talents can best be fostered within the bosom of his family. Conversely, when Buddy finds excuses not to leave home to go to college, she is pushed out by her regretful but firm family. Perhaps the one-hour form, without the cathartic relief of laughter, could not accommodate deeper anxieties about family collapse. Lacking the critical edge of the domestic comedy, the solemn family drama in the 1970s provides an imagery of harmony and consensus. But it does so only by relegating family unity to a fictive, nostalgically refurbished past, as in *The Waltons* and *Little House on the Prairie*, or by articulating tension and confusion and resolving them with internal domestic redemption, as in *Family*.

"Never underestimate the power of a story," observes British television critic Clive James. The television narrative of the 1970s begins to tell a powerful story of family trouble and dissolution. In *All in the Family* and Lear's other "ethnic comedies" the nuclear family remains formally intact but is established as the stage on which different kinds of conflict are played out—conflict about the family itself and about the meanings of family obligation, solidarity, and authority; conflict about wider social issues, structured by the key divisions of class, race, gender, and, embracing all of these, generation. The integrative, consensual tone that pervaded the shows of the 1950s and 1960s gives way to a liberal orthodoxy of pluralism, cultural diversity, and equal opportunity in the Lear comedies. Yet underlying the brassy confidence—the familiarity with events and problems pegged by a distancing, media-derived knowingness—a diffuse anger sweeps through the narratives, settling in later seasons into a pervasive anxiety, not only about family life, but also about change and modernity itself.

Comedies revolving around women tend with few exceptions to be gentler and less combative in tone; but here the family structure itself has begun to dissolve. The new heroines of situation comedy in the 1970s are typically women without men—single parents, separated or divorced rather than widowed like their counterparts in earlier years. Gathering around themselves the cobbled remnants of their own and other families' casualties, their heroism consists in fighting back, surviving alone, and developing more autonomous identities, bolstered by a particular brand of "prime-time feminism" that draws both on the energies of the women's movement and on the language and perspectives of contemporary psychology. A similar psychological sensibility permeates the sprinkling of family dramas that achieved ratings success during this period. Therapeutic language, even in shows set in the past, preserves family unity by troubleshooting internal conflict and guiding the development of family members through successive stages of the life cycle. In a decade replete with shows about fractured or troubled families, a handful of dramas provides viewers with intact, harmonious domestic lives. Yet even these either are set in visions of the past informed by Norman Rockwell and *Bonanza* or, like *Family*, incorporate a younger generation beset with splintering marriages, identity crises, and moral uncertainty.

The normative confusion and the sense of dissolving frameworks are mirrored in the changing structure of the genre. Domestic comedy in particular becomes more fluid; the neat narrative closure of 1950s comedy opens into a continuous family chronicle. With its endless parade of social problems psychologically defined and its emphasis on the ensemble of characters rather than the single star, the sitcom comes to approximate the conventions of the soap opera, a "decentered" form more appropriate to a fragmented modern sensibility. Drama jockeys for space with jokes in the 1970s comedy; the humor itself grows less zany, more a vehicle for verbal hostility and wry self-parody. It becomes harder to identify heroes and villains, and heroism itself is less a matter of winning discernible battles and attaining visible goals than of holding the fort and surviving change.

Taken together, the domestic series of prime-time television in the 1970s speak to the doubts and uncertainties of a splintered modern consciousness bewildered by the volatile changes of postwar America. In television, as in other forms of popular narrative during this period, those uncertainties surface within the family. As the following chapter shows, the dream of a harmonious, united, sustaining primary group does not disappear but is transferred from the family to the workplace.

5

All in the Work-Family
Television Families
in Workplace Settings

If the domestic hearth of television was becoming a repository for family anxiety, other, more benign images of family and community were surfacing in a subgenre designed, like the "relevant" domestic series, for affluent young urbanites within the mass audience—the television workplace series. The success of *The Mary Tyler Moore Show* and *M*A*S*H* in CBS's Saturday night lineup early in the 1970s generated a wave of series with occupational settings, such as *Lou Grant, Taxi, Barney Miller,* and *The Bob Newhart Show,* which fell into three broad formulas. In action-adventure series police and (in smaller numbers) private-detective shows returned in force to the small screen after a relative absence during the 1960s; the few one-hour dramas not concerned with law enforcement focused on prestigious occupations like medicine or journalism. Though less numerous in the top twenty than the dramatic series, the workplace comedies attracted loyal audiences over long periods of time and have proved more durable in reruns throughout the 1980s.

We have already seen that the forms and structures of television inclined toward the familial from the beginning. But *setting* is both more ambiguous and more richly charged with meaning than is innocently declared by the living rooms and kitchens of television homes. The mimetic form of the medium may convince viewers that what they see is the representation of a "real" family because the characters look familiar and because they do and say things that are plausibly familial. In Chapter 4 the consideration of shows with domestic settings demonstrated that family means more than just the kinds of homes in which people "typically" lived in 1970s America; more often than not the domestic setting becomes the repository for conflict and fear, not only about the family itself, but also about the ramifications of broader social changes for private life. The following discussion suggests that in television, *workplace* comes to express (among other things, but with particular force) an idealized construction of family, a workplace utopia whose most fulfilling attributes are vested not in work activity but in close emotional ties between coworkers. It suggests further that the episodic series, both family- and work-based, displays continuities of form and theme that, taken together, articulate anxiety about family and redeem that anxiety with a satisfying vision of family and community inserted into the professional group. The final section of the chapter examines the particular images of professionalism generated by the workplace series and their implications for public perceptions of the relationship between private and institutional worlds.

The growing emphasis on the workplace in part reflects the practical exigencies faced by producers who must routinely cast about for new ideas in order to meet network demands for endless novelty. The enclosed, obligatory environment of the workplace offers the same combination of intimacy, emotional intensity, and dramatic tension as the family group. But at a time when the family, particularly the middle-class suburban family, is perceived (at least by cultural critics) as increasingly privatized and removed from public life, the workplace opens its characters and invites its viewers to greater participation in the world outside, both organizational and beyond. In this respect the workplace offers wider possibilities than the home for advancing plot and character. Moreover, since the kinds of occupations television depicts—print and broadcast media, police work, psychotherapy—are unfamiliar to all but the tiniest minority of viewers, the television workplace offers a terrain ripe for the free play of fantasy and imaginative reconstruction, unlike the home, whose broad contours are recognizable to everyone.

A further reason for the growing prominence of the world of work in television is its potential appeal to the new kinds of audience envisioned by market demographers in the early 1970s, in particular to baby boomers preoccupied with occupational life, professional success, and "getting ahead," and to the overlapping but much larger market of women, the majority of whom were by this time working. The review in Chapter 1 of the literature on work in the 1970s suggested that although the search for meaning and community in the workplace has a long history in American culture, the concern with work and the quality of life, especially the links between work and family, takes on a new urgency with the emergence of these two groups as key constituencies within the labor force.

An unusually large generation of new college graduates faced an uncomfortable disparity between the substantial ambitions for meaningful and lucrative professions in which they had been encouraged and the employment cutbacks dictated by an unstable economy. For working women, the majority of whom were also wives and mothers, the issues were not only equality of pay and opportunity, or the more "feminized," less competitive work relationships advocated by the women's movement, but also the reconciliation of the demands of work and family life in a corporate environment largely unwilling to provide the flexibility required by most women workers. Indeed the literature suggests a serious crisis in the work ethic and a growing ambivalence toward corporate organizations, as well as a sense of confusion about the boundaries between public and private spheres, with public institutions perceived as both invasive and careless of individual or family welfare. The television workplace, which carves out a warm professional family *within* but *against* the organization, may be addressing and resolving precisely this cultural dilemma between longing for professional community and fear of the malevolent power of the corporate world.

Of course the workplace is not of interest only to middle-class baby boomers. To the mass audiences of working adults, whom television networks are anxious to retain along with the more specialized, affluent markets, the workplace must also be a central concern. Yet despite the broadening of the occupational horizons of television, the workplace shows of prime-time television in the 1970s bear scant resemblance to the experience of most Americans or to the shape of the American occupational structure. This is hardly surprising: a sizable proportion of the labor force is employed in large organizations—factories or offices; their jobs require little or no skill, creativity, or imagination and are low in pay and status, allowing less and less social interaction as automation and rationalization proceed. This is hardly the stuff of entertainment, and we are unlikely to see prime-time hits entitled *Keypunch, Assembly Line,* or *Middle Management*.[1] Despite the declared commitment of a significant minority of television producers to "realistic" entertainment, the absence of factory and clerical themes is rooted precisely in the most troubling aspects of contemporary occupational life. Routine work is boring; it is typically fragmented and lackluster, devoid of the dramatic charges of incident and interaction that enliven narrative. More than any other medium, television celebrates the ordinary, but like all imaginative narrative it must do more than simply *rehearse* the ordinary. It must heighten, dramatize, and glamorize everyday experience and offer resolution by transforming and transcending common hurts and losses, vicariously completing viewers' incomplete lives. In this sense television is both "relevant" and "escapist"; it addresses our conflicts and longings, then resolves and fulfills them.

This combination of the dramatic and the quotidian may help to explain why the majority of television workplaces in the 1970s are the sites of potentially glamorous professions but are decrepit or second-rate examples of these professions. Peopling an exciting occupation with eccentrics of modest achievement turns the television workplace into a compromise between the exhilaration of upward mobility, social power, and prestige on the one hand, and the populist affirmation of ordinariness on the other. This is not to say that producers wrote their scripts with such complex goals in mind. Indeed, to judge by the comments of James Brooks, senior writer for MTM Productions, which specialized in workplace series, some producers may have been writing television versions of their own work situations, which both celebrated the collaborative intimacy of television production and voiced their resentment toward the media and advertisers on whom they depended.[2] The choice of media occupations by MTM producers for the settings of their series supports this view. Indeed Paul Kerr (1984) draws interesting parallels between MTM producers' perceptions of the fate of their company in the 1970s as the transformation of a "cozy family business" into a faceless corporation, and the decidedly anticorporate sensibility of their shows. In this way the television workplace of the 1970s can gratify the presumed wishes of both upscale and mass audiences at the same time as it articulates the profound ambivalence about corporate and professional institutions indicated by cultural criticism during this period.

If Norman Lear's Tandem set the tone for domestic comedy during this period, Grant Tinker's MTM Productions pioneered the format for the workplace series. One of the best-loved comedies of the decade, *The Mary Tyler Moore Show*, established the company's reputation (and in the 1980s that of NBC, for whom MTM produced most of its shows) for "quality television" and set the tone for a succession of workplace comedies with a distinctive MTM house style. By gearing its material to the smaller but more affluent audiences in the 18–49 age group, and by balancing current losses against future profits from syndication, the company was able to make quality pay and establish a reputation for "different" programming that coincided with the changing commercial priorities of the networks. Jane Feuer's (1984) analysis of the MTM house style argues that the "liberal-realist" character comedies pioneered by writers such as James Brooks and Allan Burns produced a modernist sensibility whose mild, self-reflexive satire fell well within the economic imperatives of an industry bent on reaping the fruits of advertising revenue generated by wealthier, better-educated viewers. But the meanings of MTM shows extend far beyond the congruence of house style with commercial priorities, into a resonance with particular currents of social change. Feuer offers a double reading of the MTM work-family, which in her view mythologizes the workplace as an arena of intimacy and harmony but also holds out a vision of alternatives to the nuclear family, especially for women. The liberal structure of the typical MTM series, according to Feuer, makes room for multiple readings, which may explain in part the appeal of the MTM shows for a broad range of viewers.

Like *All in the Family*, *The Mary Tyler Moore Show* received a good deal of critical and other media attention, though more for its aesthetic merits (scriptwriting and acting) than for its social commentary. There is little doubt, however, that the show's popularity derived in part from its star, who as Rob Petrie's pretty helpmeet Laura on *The Dick Van Dyke Show* had built a loyal following among viewers. Some of Laura Petrie is sustained in Moore's second television persona. Sweet, conventional, accommodating, and self-effacing, Mary Richards ought by rights to have married a successful professional and hung her frilly curtains in the New Rochelle suburban home that Laura had so blissfully inhabited. But in common with many women of her generation, Mary's life plans have not worked out; following the failure of a long relationship with a medical student who reneges on his promise to marry her when his training is completed, the thirty-year-old woman arrives in Minneapolis to begin a new life.[3] Searching for secretarial work, she finds a job at WJM, a homespun television station where her honorary title of assistant producer on the nightly news show allows her wily boss, Lou Grant, to pay her less than a secretary's salary and use her as a girl Friday. "I wonder why he hired me?" she frets to her desk mate Murray, frustrated at not being taken seriously. "Don't you know?" he answers gleefully, "You're our token woman!"

The Mary Tyler Moore Show is not the first television comedy to center around an unmarried woman. In *Our Miss Brooks* the title character, played by Eve Arden, organized her life around an unflagging campaign to ensnare a fellow teacher and lead him to the altar, and Marlo Thomas, in *That Girl,* played a nice "girl" with a steady boyfriend who never stayed the night. Mary too would like to find a husband, but she is far from desperate and takes her work very seriously. Battling daily with Lou's careless prejudice and her own insecurities (Mary: "You have to be able to exert authority, and I can't do that. They're probably not even going to listen to me!" Lou: "What's that you say?") she becomes much more than a token, rising to associate producer and then producer of the nightly news. Still, Mary Richards remains Laura Petrie dropped unceremoniously into a new and confusing world without the security of suburban home, husband, and family. Like many women in their thirties, and like the women of the domestic comedies, Mary must make her way alone, negotiating job and home, friends and lovers, in a world dominated by men and without rules for guidance.

The Mary Tyler Moore Show inherits the work-home duality of *The Dick Van Dyke Show*. But if the setting is the same, its meaning is not. Rob Petrie was on the way up, part of a successful television comedy writing team. WJM is a haphazard local news operation at a third-rate television station. Rob returned home each evening to a storybook nuclear family. Mary comes home to a "bachelor" studio with a sofabed, and her intimates are her neighbor Rhoda Morgenstern, a vivacious Jewish window dresser from New York who is also single, and their posturing landlady Phyllis Lindstrom, a caricature of the well-heeled suburban matron with too much time on her hands. This is no tale of a lonely spinster, though. The weekly opening sequence offers its own narrative— shots of Mary striding along by a pond, glancing over her shoulder with decorous lust at a pair of jogging men; Mary disgustedly tossing a small "singles" package of frozen food into her basket at the supermarket; Mary rushed and disheveled in the elevator; and finally, Mary arriving "home" at the office, joyously hugging each of her colleagues, then throwing her hat jubilantly in the air. "How will you make it on your own? This world is awfully big . . . " begins the title song, but it ends, "You're gonna make it after all." Gutsy, cheerful survival will be the new heroism of the single working woman, just as it is for the new heroines of domestic comedy in the 1970s.

Mary's family life, then, is carried on at work among her newsroom colleagues—Lou Grant, her brusque, hard-drinking boss; Murray Slaughter, the comfortable, balding newswriter, who represents Everyman in every respect but his wisecracking wit; Ted Baxter, a walking send-up of the narcissistic television anchorman, whose looks suggest a handsome, white-haired patriarch but who is childish, self-absorbed, and dim-witted; and Sue Ann Nivens, the host of a cooking show (*The Happy Homemaker*), whose sugary, respectable-matron smile barely conceals a voracious and undiscriminating sexual appetite. Mary's apartment comes to serve as an annex, a haven for her work-family, whose members drop in at will. Lou haunts her apartment nightly for weeks after his wife leaves him, expecting to be cared for by his "office wife." Ted's wife Georgette goes into labor and the baby is delivered by Mary and Lou (the parents name her Mary Lou). When Mary's insomnia threatens to turn into a dependency on sleeping pills, Lou sings her to sleep on her own sofa and sits there all night without moving for fear of waking her. Mary grows temporarily restless, feeling she is in a rut; rather than leave her job, she moves to a new apartment. The lines between home and work and between Mary's roles in each sphere grow hazier as the series progresses. Rhoda and Phyllis are gradually drawn into the life of the WJM work-family. Ted proposes to his girlfriend Georgette on television ("What do you think of this big impetuous lug?" croons the ecstatic Georgette, a Gracie Allen–type ingenue, "popping the question between a nuclear war and a flea collar commercial!").

By all the criteria of worldly success WJM is a failure, its production team at best modestly competent, at worst hopeless bunglers. Though they are skilled at covering stories about drowning kittens, the WJM staffers are always last with the big news. In love and work they suffer the daily disappointments of being average (each is regularly passed over for dubious recognition at the tacky local television awards ceremonies) and the weightier disasters of divorce and abandonment, unrequited love, mid-life crises, and the ever-present specter of unemployment. An ailing television station encapsulates the tarnished glamor of a fading American Dream—a fitting image for the economic and status anxieties of the 1970s. It also renders the glamorous ordinary, and the ordinary glamorous, in ways that can excite viewers without threatening them.

But Mary and her crew of average oddballs excel as a self-sustaining humanistic collective. As with domestic comedy, what "happens" routinely at WJM serves less to push along and tie up events than to develop viewer attachment to the characters and cement their relationships to one another, individually and as a group. What goes on "outside" (whether in love, family, or work) is drawn into, and resolved within, the WJM family; the group infuses the suffering individual with the strength to survive. Success is redefined as the ability to weather adversity, to fight back, and to carry on. Their unity is more than just the chummy fraternity of colleagues, shed when they leave the office: it defines their existence. The WJM newsroom has the hierarchy and emotional intensity of a family. Mary is by turns mother, daughter, and competitive sibling in her work-family. Always trying but never able to break her habit of addressing Lou as Mr. Grant, she is equally likely to mother him and the others when the occasion arises. As their boss and paterfamilias, Lou in time discards his blustery autocracy for a gentler leadership; he remains grumpy but becomes more flexible, democratic, and loving. The solid core of Mary's life, indeed of all the characters' lives as well as the viewers' attention and allegiance, is work "with the family." Until the famous final episode, in which everyone except Ted is fired, it is virtually the only constant in lives otherwise governed by change and uncertainty and by nasty surprises that are often the unintended consequences of their own actions. The work-family in *The Mary Tyler Moore Show* is the powerful center into which character and event, and viewer attention, are drawn. The workplace becomes the stage on which what is most significant and emotionally redeeming about everyday life occurs.

But if WJM provides a primary haven of love and shelter, it also crackles with the hostility and ambivalence that form the other side of the coin of family intimacy. Mary and Murray get along beautifully as long as they do different jobs. But when Lou promotes Murray to associate producer in order to head off his defection to another television station, making him equal in rank and responsibility to Mary, she must fight (unsuccessfully) to contain her mounting resentment. Murray and Sue Ann pursue a gleeful war of attrition, each trying to cap the other's insults. Sue Ann fires off backhanded salvos about Mary's propriety. Ted is an emotionally fragile child, manipulative, eternally jealous of others' achievements, his precarious equilibrium shattered at a stroke; he whines to Lou when he feels left out. But however much he might infuriate and enrage the others, they cannot bear to see him go. When he is offered a job appropriate to his talents, as quizmaster on an infantile game show in New York, one by one his colleagues sheepishly beg him to stay. "You couldn't leave us," pleads Mary, "this is your home!" "You're right," agrees Ted happily, "this is where my friends are, the people that love me." But when the phone rings a second later, he mutters, "Maybe this is my ticket out of this dump!" *The Mary Tyler Moore Show* has plenty of aggression, but its frisky hostilities contrast sharply with the undifferentiated rage boiling over in *All in the Family* or *The Jeffersons;* there is never a sense that the unit itself is threatened with dissolution, except from without.

As the seasons wear on (*The Mary Tyler Moore Show* flourished for seven years and remains a popular rerun in syndication) the WJM work-family consolidates its exclusivity. Lou's wife Edie leaves him in order to "find herself." After twenty-six years of married life Lou is unaccustomed to introspection, and his first response is to transfer his domestic needs wholesale to Mary. Each evening he presents his tubby, careworn self at her door for dinner as if nothing were amiss, cajoling her into the role of go-between with his wife and issuing terse progress reports through Mary to his other colleagues ("Not bad; not good. Pass it on"). Murray and Mary play key advisory and supportive roles in Lou's adjustment to divorce and to Edie's remarriage, and in his subsequent romances. Moreover, they feel his pain: Mary sobs uncontrollably throughout Edie's marriage ceremony and continues to cry with Lou and Murray in their local bar afterward. In conversation with Mary, Lou confesses shamefacedly to a fling with Sue Ann. When Mary leaks his secret to Murray, Lou is driven to waving above her distraught head the one threat she cannot bear to hear: they can continue as colleagues but not as friends. Lou dates Mary's feisty journalist aunt Flo, and it is Mary who picks up the pieces when his clumsy marriage proposal to her aunt is turned down. His relationship with a barroom singer runs into difficulties; the lovers turn to Mary for advice and consolation. Thus the increasingly problematic and unpredictable world of love and marriage is redeemed by the reliable solidarity of the workplace gemeinschaft.

Mary's own love life (like that of her friend Rhoda) is, if anything, more frustrating and unfulfilled than that of her boss. Monitored by her hypercritical and protective colleagues, she dates a succession of limp, feckless wimps, gorgeous but brainless hunks, and attractive but undependable or unavailable men. Again and again Mary's search for the right man is thwarted. she is stood up or rejected by unreliable men or slavishly adored by suitors for whom she can muster little more than pity. Mary Richards is the model for that resonant figure of the 1970s and early 1980s (not only in television but also in film and popular fiction)—the incomplete woman.[4]

In a rare episode in which she does date a man she thinks she can love, Mary is plunged into a lather of uncertainty about how to act. Why doesn't Joe tell her he loves her? Should she take the initiative? Rhoda, who is more forward than her proper friend, advocates a pragmatic honesty: "In this day and age that's the only thing for a woman to do . . . assuming trickery and deceit have already failed!" Mary musters all her courage and arrives unannounced at Joe's apartment, only to discover him with another woman. Covered in confusion, she takes refuge in the conventions she knows and exchanges polite small talk with the woman. "Mary, we have a situation on our hands!" exclaims the baffled and embarrassed Joe. "I know," wails Mary, "I just haven't the vaguest idea how to deal with it!" Torn between her desire to be "modern" and her hurt feelings, she makes a valiant stab at being cool ("You and I have no special commitment to each other"), then bursts out, "How could you do this to me?" Joe explains that this is the way he is and tells her he loves her; having little room to maneuver, Mary cheerfully makes do.

Mary dates her journalism class teacher but becomes infuriated when he gives her, the only professional in the class, a grade of C plus for her assignment. She is further outraged when he sees no reason to stop going out with her ("I've gone out with C plus's before"). Mary dates Murray's father against all advice, including her colleagues' jealous disapproval. Having made an impassioned speech in front of a party full of guests about her right to go out with whomever she pleases, she finds herself gently dumped. Worse still, her successor is a woman of her own age, an old friend whom Mr. Slaughter has decided to marry. She rejects a manipulative television critic who will withdraw a grossly distorted interview only if she agrees to sleep with him. But she is unsure of her judgment and consults her best friend: "Rhoda, do you think I'm undersexed?" In a parody of obsolete romantic counseling Rhoda assures her that "you did the right thing . . . he was just testing to see what kind of a girl you are . . . he'll call you." Mary brightens: "Do you think so?" "No," says Rhoda, "but my mother does!" Pat answers and clearcut sexual mores will no longer serve for the dilemmas that plague Mary and Rhoda (as well as their counterparts Maude and Ann Romano and Gloria Bunker in the domestic comedies) and must carry a disturbing charge for married and single women viewers alike; they flounder along, improvising rules and defending their dignity with self-deprecating jokes.

The Mary Tyler Moore Show is a comedy of unintended consequences and embarrassment. Faced with new or uncertain situations without clear rules for action, its characters suffer orgies of discomfort, even humiliation, as they strive to preserve face. Mary is the queen of embarrassment and outrage. (Indeed her creator, James Brooks, has become an auteur of the comedy of embarrassment; his 1987 film *Broadcast News* relies on the peculiarly modern humor that takes normatively inappropriate behavior as its text.) Time after time she finds herself in situations that have spun out of control—not, as in *I Love Lucy*, because of a misunderstanding or accident the viewer knows will shortly be set right, but because the rules of everyday social interaction are confused or simply unknown. Mary does not know how to act; nor do we, since more often than not the narrative offers only a resigned accommodation by way of resolution.

Mary repeatedly is let down, her dreams shattered, but she is philosophical and keeps bouncing back for more. In the penultimate episode of the show's final season she begins to despair of ever finding a suitable partner. A boorish date removes his shirt the moment he enters her apartment, and an uncharacteristically furious Mary spills out the accumulated frustration of two thousand dates, which, she bitterly calculates, add up to twenty years of dating:

I am thinking of all the rituals, and for what? All the hours spent getting through the evening . . . I mean I have just had it with all these games, over and over again, I'm too old for this!

In a calmer mood she confesses her fears to a sympathetic Georgette:

You know how you go along thinking some day you'll meet the right person. Well, for the first time I'm not sure that's going to happen . . . I'm not sure he even exists . . . I didn't think I was asking for that much, but I haven't met anyone who even comes close. Someone who doesn't care how I look, because he's more concerned with who I am . . . somebody strong and intelligent . . . who respects me, who I can respect . . . who has gentleness in him. I guess there just aren't any men like that.

Desperate and egged on by Georgette, Mary breaks a long-standing taboo and asks Lou out on a date. As a romantic event, Mary's intimate candlelight dinner is a comic disaster, a study in uncertainty, discomfort, and ambivalence. For the viewer, who has come to know Mary and Lou as both daughter/father and mother/son, it is an entirely predictable disaster, yet the progression from its first airing as a possibility to its inevitable decline into failure is compelling; there is satisfaction in seeing the prospect of romance raised and then punctured. The tension of their tantalizing but dangerous liaison (dangerous not merely because they work together but because it signifies a kind of father/daughter incest) breaks when they attempt a kiss, collapsing midway into giggles, then settle comfortably into gossip about what happened at work during the day. "At work" is the life that is reassuringly known, its rules tacitly understood and followed. Mary's search for a man can never be as frantic or as disappointing as that of *Our Miss Brooks* because she leads a rich and complex emotional life at work.

If WJM has the concentrated exclusivity of a family, it also harbors the forbidden attractions of kinship. Mary's single state, together with the complexities of her personality and her style of womanhood, provide the erotic trigger to her male colleagues' fantasies but also serve to curb them. First, she is the homecoming queen ("You're not the kind of girl a guy brings gin to," reflects Lou). She has about her an air of the incorporeal madonna ("Somehow I never pictured Mary as having garbage," says Murray.) But she also becomes the New Woman, sexy and increasingly assured in her dealings with men in work and love. Mary's abortive date with Lou is one of several episodes that toys with, but never realizes, her attraction for the others. An early episode has Lou, Ted, and Murray dreaming, with the rapturous abandon that fantasy allows, about what it would be like to be married to Mary. In another, Murray, who is happily married but always agonizes about his mundane life, who rushes away early from a glamorous convention in California because his daughter's pet hamster is "lethargic," finally gives voice to the holy passion he feels for Mary. And Ted, in his infinite vanity, is convinced that the merest crook of his little finger will bring Mary running.

If this continuity, these indestructible loyalties unconditionally given, accounts for the enormous success of *The Mary Tyler Moore Show,* so too does its other voice, a pervasive tone of ambiguity and ambivalence that opens the show to multiple, often divergent readings and that fans out from personal to professional relations and obligations. Here the show's disclaiming humor thrusts an edge of uncertainty into every declared commitment. Lou announces solemnly that he is not empowered to give Mary the day off to go to her high-school reunion, but he advises her to "do like I do and call in sick." Mary asks her aunt Flo, a journalist of national repute, how she acquired some confidential information and receives the gleeful reply, "Let's just say it was a combination of arm twisting, bribery, and deceit . . . all the tools that we reporters employ to safeguard democracy!" Unlike the domestic comedies of Norman Lear, in which anger and ambivalence gather strength and chip away at the foundations of the family, the rifts and hostilities at WJM never undermine the integrity of the group. Conflict is almost invariably harmonized, and unity happily reaffirmed, by the end of an episode. So too with the cynicism about work norms, which belies a fundamental (if sometimes reluctant) commitment to professional honesty. When Ted compromises his "dignity" as a newsman by doing commercials on the side, he brings down the collective fury of his colleagues on his head.

Mary is the show's ethical straight-woman, its symbol of an outmoded idealism cast aside by a world in which success requires duplicity and self-advertisement. She goes to jail rather than reveal her sources. She resigns when Lou prints a damaging story about a congressman who is an old friend of hers. And when Lou's capacity for exploitation and deviousness grows too much for her (as it frequently does), there is her familiar, exasperated wail, "Mr. Grant!" Mary keeps her colleagues honest, but, repeatedly outmaneuvered, she also forces us to face the impotence of her values outside her immediate environment. With its old-fashioned integrity, WJM functions as a moral oasis in an institutional world bereft of moral perspective. It is an oasis doomed to perish since in the last show, portending the rationalization of the television station, everyone except the supremely ungifted and amoral Ted is fired. Yet we are invited to endorse the persistence of the ethics of the "classical" professions in a corporate world from which ethics and the humane concern for others have been evacuated.

Like its warm family imagery, the edgy ambiguity of *The Mary Tyler Moore Show* may be a part of its appeal. It feeds our contemporary ambivalence—our confusion about where to place our loyalties, about which values and institutions are to be trusted, and about change itself. If the thrust of each episode positions us to identify with Mary's growing competence and assurance and her maturity as a woman, it also carries an undertow of misogyny. Indeed *The Mary Tyler Moore Show* is almost as likely to appeal to antifeminists as it is to feminists. Mary's rise from secretary at WJM to producer of her own show, her solid friendships with Rhoda and Georgette, her resistance to Lou's cunning manipulations, and her growing self-confidence in dealing with men provide a steady theme of women's independence and self-awareness. Still, she remains the hometown girl in an arbitrary world that contrives with alarming regularity not simply to thwart but also to embarrass and humiliate her. When Mary's show flops or her date stands her up for the twentieth time, the viewer can either laugh at her or with her, or both. Mary is simultaneously heroine and whipping girl.

Similar ambiguities mark the other women characters: Georgette, Ted's reedy-voiced girlfriend, who enters the series as an obtuse blonde bimbo but grows into a principled woman, sustaining Ted but standing up to his more egregious displays of selfishness or cowardice; Sue Ann, whose vibrating waterbed, another accoutrement in her search for the ultimate hunk, provokes roars of audience laughter not just because she is a woman but because she is middle-aged (the implication is that she no longer is supposed to be interested in sex); and Rhoda, who introduces herself as "Mary's good-natured friend Rhoda." Echoing the domestic series, nearly every show hedges its bets with a variety of women characters—daffy, man-eating, frustrated, pretentious, honest, achieving—that run the gamut from traditional to modern. There is something for everyone: the formula allows the viewer to identify with the "new woman" while hanging onto older ideals of femininity, and retains for the show its male audience. If in the end our sympathies are guided definitively toward these women, it is because they triumph over a fearful battering by dint of cheerful survival, not because they have fully attained their more concrete goals. By the final episode Mary still has not found a partner, and she has been fired. Hers is a liberation at the level of consciousness and positive attitude rather than attainment.

The Mary Tyler Moore Show is a subtler, sweeter, gentler show than the other smash hit of CBS's 1971 Saturday night lineup, *All in the Family*. Its "relevance," as James Brooks was well aware, lies more in the contemporaneity of its characters' daily lives than in the exploration of formally defined issues. Still, it shares with *All in the Family* the ability to appeal to several kinds of audiences at once. The combination in Mary of girl-next-door sweetness and "old-fashioned" attachment to honesty and integrity, on the one hand, and achieving, spunky New Woman, on the other, allows *The Mary Tyler Moore Show* to ride the currents of social change, endorsing modernity at the same time as it hallows tradition. As Serafina

Bathrick (1984) suggests in her essay on the series, *The Mary Tyler Moore Show* addresses the postwar shift from the ideal of the "domestic True Woman" to that of the "career True Woman," pulling us in different directions through Mary's mediating skills at home and work. At home Mary and friends offer a vision of sisterly solidarity, community, and cooperation, an alternative to the hierarchical authority of the nuclear family. At work they also generate community, proposing a familial alternative in which friendship rather than kinship acts as the primary social bond. Yet here the more traditional gender roles they play as daughters, sisters, and mothers undercut their (frequently ridiculed) professional skills and harmonize role conflicts that in everyday life prove much less tractable. Mary Richards becomes the "career True Woman" as a television producer who nonetheless retains the equable charm and mediating skills of the well–brought-up girl. This is a difficult reconciliation to pull off in life, and therefore it is very satisfying—for men as well as women—to see on the small screen.

These conflicts reassert themselves in *Rhoda*, a spinoff from *The Mary Tyler Moore Show*, which in its later seasons came to focus on Rhoda's work as a window dresser and interior designer. One sequence of episodes, "Rhoda Nine to Five," examines the vicissitudes of a woman at work, and here its tone is self-consciously feminist (many scripts were partly or wholly written by women). Established at last in her own business, Rhoda negotiates the diplomatic and strategic uncertainties of doing business in a man's world. Her new landlord wants her lease to be signed by her husband Joe; Rhoda insists on signing, and in her own name. She pays the man who delivers sandwiches, and he returns the change to Joe. Joe maintains he is supportive of her venture—until it keeps her late at the office. Her assistant Myrna is in the habit of winning new accounts by dating prospective clients; Rhoda is appalled, concerned both about the dubious business ethics of such behavior and about her friend's vulnerability to exploitation. "Why can't you have a business relationship with a man without the fact that you're a woman gets in the way?" she complains to her sister Brenda. Brenda is sympathetic but reminds her that at the bank where she works the prettiest tellers are placed in the most visible positions.

Determined nonetheless to prove her point, Rhoda sets off to collar an account with a client and encounters exactly the sort of treatment she had feared. When she accidentally topples and smashes a pile of plates, the client says, "That's O.K., you're cute, you can get away with it!" Frustrated and angry, Rhoda loses her temper—"I wanted to believe that there are still people doing business without getting some action on the side"—to which her protagonist complacently replies, "There's always something sexual going on between a man and a woman." They part in hostility, but Rhoda, unable to let matters rest, returns to have her say: "You know what's crummy is, you never looked at my sketches!" Grudgingly he looks, and he likes them; Rhoda has won the account on her own terms.

There is also another kind of ambiguity in these shows. Though Mary is the star, the *The Mary Tyler Moore Show* has no single perspective. She works within an ensemble; indeed her role is often reactive, and her looks of outrage, shock, surprise, and delight serve to sharpen and define the other characters. And if the group, the work-family, is of primary importance, so too are its individual members. Far more than in *I Love Lucy* or *The Dick Van Dyke Show* the viewer's attention and allegiance are shunted from one character to another. The narrative is less linear and the characters decentered, creating a world more relativistic and less clearly demarcated into good and evil. If the television narrative is again having it both ways, celebrating both individual freedom and group solidarity, its underlying meanings suggest that only in the group, specifically the professional group, can the individual clarify his or her identity.

The Mary Tyler Moore Show proposes television as family—not just Mary's family but the viewers' too. In so doing, it recasts the hierarchical boundaries not only of the television world but of the work world in general. The cozy, domestic "inside" harbors a family of folksy professionals doing the best they can without benefit of power, status, or formal training. Television's rendering of "professionalism" makes an ideological virtue out of the necessity of coping, of muddling along against the odds. And the odds are generated, as often as not, by the "outside"—the executives and station owners, variously depicted as stupid, authoritarian, or in-effectual, who control television and make life difficult for those who have to do the practical work. Both WJM's stammering station manager and its owner, a demented would-be cowboy who rides a rocking horse in his office, casually deploy power in uninformed, arbitrary, and abstract ways that nonetheless have profound and often damaging effects on the lives of their staff.

Striking similarities of form and theme are evident in another CBS hit comedy (though in this case not from MTM Productions), *M*A*S*H*. When the series first aired in 1972, its overall ratings were poor, but the demographics showed that it was very popular among young adults, perhaps because of its explicitly antiauthoritarian stance. Once CBS's Fred Silverman had slotted it into the Saturday night lineup between *All in the Family* and *The Mary Tyler Moore Show* in the fall of 1973, the series leaped into the top ten and stayed there. By the measures of ratings success and longevity alone, *M*A*S*H* ranks as the all-time hit comedy in television. The series played for a total of eleven years in prime time, occupying a place in the top ten through most of that period, and is kept alive today in syndication.[5]

The creator of *M*A*S*H*, veteran comedy writer Larry Gelbart, took the premise and character of Robert Altman's 1970 movie, a savage satire on war and its profiteers set in a mobile army emergency surgical unit during the Korean War, and tamed it for prime-time television. He eliminated the violence, humanized the characters, and watered down the antiwar sentiment to a more oblique pacifism. "We wanted to say that war was futile, to represent it as a failure on everybody's part that people had to kill each other to make a point," Gelbart told an interviewer. "We tended to make the war the enemy without really saying who was fighting. . . . It was chic to be anti-war. . . . You couldn't offend anybody" (quoted in Gitlin 1985, 217).

M*A*S*H is far from the first military comedy in television history. In shows like *The Phil Silvers Show*, *McHale's Navy*, and *Hogan's Heroes* the army and navy had proved popular settings for wacky sitcoms. *M*A*S*H*'s Southeast Asian setting of course carried a special charge for early 1970s viewers caught up in the Vietnam War and its aftermath. But despite its diffuse pacifism, the show inherits a good deal of the rapid-fire banter and schoolboy prankishness of its antecedents. It begins as a boys-on-the-loose sitcom, focusing on the antics of two frisky young surgeons, Hawkeye Pierce and Trapper John McIntyre, who, when not tending the wounded, devote themselves to the energetic pursuit of drink and nurses, and bait their stuffy, inept colleague, Frank Burns, and his lover, Margaret "Hotlips" Houlihan.

As the series unfolds, the bantering exchange of one-liners and plotty capers become integrated into fuller stories of everyday life; like others of its genre, *M*A*S*H* turns into a chronicle. The show achieves a more serious tone, mixing comedy and drama, not just about the war itself, but more centrally about the emotional and psychological development of its ensemble of characters. The viewer's attention broadens out from Hawkeye and Trapper John to the 4077th Mobile Army Surgical Hospital unit as a whole. Three important casting changes accelerated the domestication of the *M*A*S*H* "family," sharpening the differentiation of its characters and knitting them into a structured primary group. In 1975 Trapper John was replaced by B. J. Hunnicutt, a happily married, mellow Californian so different from Hawkeye that the boyish bonding between Hawkeye and Trapper deepened in this new relationship into a more reciprocal, brotherly camaraderie. The doltish, malleable Henry Blake, who initially headed the 4077th, was replaced by Colonel Sherman Potter, whose firm, democratic leadership and practical flexibility with regard to the application of rules combined with his avuncular concern to make him the kind of doctor, the kind of leader, and the kind of father anyone might wish for, especially under stressful conditions. Frank Burns, self-serving and incompetent for all his slavish adherence to army regulations and lacking the redeeming traits necessary to enlist audience sympathy, went permanently AWOL and was succeeded by the fastidious Charles Winchester, a Boston Brahmin and therefore a sitting target for much populist derision, but who like the others was a dedicated surgeon and loyal friend when the chips were down.

Deprived of her clownish, unprepossessing lover, Margaret too is freed to grow into a more independent and likable head nurse. Her frequent flings with visiting military personnel, a short-lived marriage, and a brief liaison with Hawkeye establish both her desirability and (echoing the situation of Mary Richards) her untouchability for the M.A.S.H. unit, which is strengthened by the filial affection and respect she shows toward Colonel Potter. Potter indeed treats all the surgeons as his children, cheering them on when they are down, pulling them back into line when they stray, protecting them from their own follies and the arbitrary power of army bigwigs. When B. J. and Winchester quarrel and compete over a research paper they have coauthored, Potter reminds them of higher loyalties—"This kind of recognition could benefit us all—put those egos in neutral!"—and he persuades them to submit the paper as a collective effort of the 4077th M.A.S.H. unit.

Each member of the unit has a special relationship with Radar O'Reilly, the Colonel's aide, whom they tease unmercifully but nurture and protect. Radar acts the bashful adolescent prone to teen talk ("None of your beeswax!"), retreating into a jealous sulk when Potter (who habitually addresses him as "son") neglects him to spend time with a visiting woman colonel. But he is also a fussy housewife who knows where everything is and clucks with disapproval when someone upsets his filing system. The addition of Corporal Klinger, with his propensity for wearing dresses and makeup, bends the elastic gender boundaries of *M*A*S*H* still further and also provides a satirical yet sympathetic commentary on well-publicized strategies for avoiding shipment to Vietnam. At the same time it adds to the larky ambience that proposes life at the 4077th, and by extension both the army and the war, as a romp. The ramshackle sets, Hawkeye and B. J.'s chaotic tent ("the Swamp"), their pillow fights and practical jokes, and their friendly rivalries transform the surgical unit into a summer camp.

As *M*A*S*H* grows into a family, the war becomes a secondary concern or is woven into narratives that center on the personal problems of different members of the unit. Klinger abandons female dress and accordingly becomes less of a caricature and more of a fully rounded character with serious concerns of his own. Many episodes rehearse Hawkeye's struggle to mediate between his cynicism and his humanity as he tries to gain perspective on the war and life in general. Potter and B. J. respectively are tempted into extramarital affairs, which they both resist. Margaret moves toward a more considered identity as an independent woman. For counseling they all have each other, Colonel Potter, and Father Mulcahy, the gentle but worldly chaplain. But as their problems acquire a more psychological and developmental cast, it is psychiatrist Sidney Friedman who becomes the unit's emotional troubleshooter, signifying the triumph of psychotherapeutic over religious authority. Colonel Potter makes a mistake in surgery and is plunged into anxiety about growing old; Sidney talks down his denial and gets him to face his fears. Hawkeye develops an unaccountable sneezing habit, and Sidney traces it back to the repressed trauma of a childhood boating accident. Yet as with many other shows during this period, the endorsement of a therapeutic perspective is undercut by a bantering cynicism about the efficacy of psychology and the professionals who practice it.

The continuous core of the *M*A*S*H* narrative is its provision of a warm, safe, and loving sanctuary in the middle of a chaotic and unpredictable world that operates through arbitrary and pointless authority. The rules of the outside world are suspended at the 4077th: doctors wear Hawaiian shirts, joke as they perform surgery, and indulge in pillow fights and other childish pranks. Gender definitions are loose and malleable, with men weaving in and out of female roles and providing more nurturant, womanly styles of authority. The rules on the "inside" prescribe tolerance of eccentricity, love, solidarity, devotion to the healing, and protection of the weak.

As with *The Mary Tyler Moore Show*, part of the continuing appeal of *M*A*S*H* for its audiences may lie in the ambiguity and contradictory nature of its meanings. War is wrong, it clearly says, but it is either nobody's fault or everybody's fault. "Damn Truman, damn Stalin, damn everybody!" shouts Klinger in frustration. Contradictions are reconciled or resolved; the army is the place where the whims of despots must be suffered, but life in it is like Spree Day at Scout camp. A soldier may romance a colleague and be true to a wife who lives conveniently far away. Being a surgeon is serious, a terrible responsibility, a frightening experience—and a lot of fun.

Other successful comedies soon echoed the home-in-the-workplace format of *The Mary Tyler Moore Show* and *M*A*S*H*. MTM Productions in particular developed a house style that lodged its work-families in middle-range occupations that nevertheless are resonant and appealing in contemporary American culture—print and broadcast media, psychotherapy, sports—using them to satirize and also to humanize those occupations. Here too the work-family carves out an intimate, sheltering space within the organization, redeeming the impersonality and arbitrariness of institutional life.

In 1972 *The Bob Newhart Show,* a sitcom featuring comedian Bob Newhart as a psychologist presiding over a therapy group consisting of assorted neurotics and lost souls, joined the CBS Saturday night lineup, where it was to enjoy six successful seasons; it continues to thrive in syndication. Like *The Mary Tyler Moore Show, The Bob Newhart Show* comments satirically on its professional setting. Bob Hartley is blessed with the kind of success attributed to some psychotherapists; he has a steady cadre of patients, none of whom is ever cured. The boundaries between his life at work and his life at home with schoolteacher wife Emily are indistinct. Though the Hartleys are childless, they care for a large brood of "children" who, aside from their neighbor Howard, a divorced airline pilot with the bemused air and giggly awkwardness of a boy entering adolescence, are all connected with Bob's practice. Bob's life with Emily serves as a site for mulling over what goes on at the office, whether between Bob, his secretary Carol, and his office mate Jerry, an orthodontist, or with his therapy group.

Bob's therapeutic technique fails abysmally when he is at his most intellectual and abstract. When he mouths the clichés of contemporary psychology in the flat, unconvinced monotone that made Newhart the comedian famous ("Go with that thought, Mrs. Bakerman!") he is either ignored or dumped on by his patients. But he excels as a nurturing mother figure—taking care of them, giving them commonsense advice, throwing a party for them on Christmas Eve, protecting them from the outside world and their own families. His therapy group is at once a microcosm of an outside world perceived as crazy and a refuge for the casualties of that world. His two colleagues, Jerry and Carol, are only marginally less loony than his patients and no less dependent on Bob, as he is on them.

MTM's other successful media comedy, *WKRP in Cincinnati,* rushed to the top of the ratings in 1979 as a summer rerun and, like others of its kind, survives through the 1980s in syndication. The show virtually reproduces the format of *The Mary Tyler Moore Show,* translating it into a top-forty radio station newly converted from "beautiful music" to rock and roll so that it combines an appeal for teenage audiences with the hip, sarcastic banter of young urban adults. Headed by the amiable but ineffectual Mr. Carlson, who bumbles along happily when he is not being terrorized by his draconian mother (the station's owner), WKRP is saved from extinction by its hardworking, hip young station manager, Andy Travis, and by the unifying culture of rock and roll. If WKRP pays tribute to the radical politics of the counterculture through popular music, it also tames this opposition by situating the pop generation inside that most traditional of institutions, a family. Andy's time is largely spent trying to orchestrate and control the unruly tribe of more or less lovable cranks and eccentrics who staff WKRP; as with *The Mary Tyler Moore Show*, it is the everyday life of this ensemble of "average crackpots" that knits together the narrative. WKRP is short on funds, technology, glitter, and ratings success, but it has love, tolerance, and support aplenty, and the eternal bickering of its "children" sustains its domestic, quotidian tone.

Later in the decade other companies were able to capitalize on the success of *M*A*S*H* and *The Mary Tyler Moore Show* by producing workplace comedies for receptive network executives. ABC's *Taxi*, though not officially an MTM creation, was written by a group of veteran MTM writers. Undoubtedly the series, set in the down-at-heel garage of the Sunshine Cab Company, bears the MTM stamp—a collection of disheveled oddballs, recognizable social types welded into a family by their common work situation and by the insufficiency of their personal lives outside the workplace. ABC's *Barney Miller*, one of the few police comedies in prime time, takes place in the headquarters of Greenwich Village's Twelfth Precinct, which offers a fertile stamping ground for the procession of social rejects and kooks who parade through the dingy but cozy offices of Captain Barney Miller and his squad of detectives. CBS's *Alice* takes from the movie *Alice Doesn't Live Here Any More* the premise of a widowed, aspiring singer supporting herself and her son by working in a cafe. In the television version Alice's life revolves more around her fellow workers in the cafe than around her singing career. And ABC's *Welcome Back Kotter* returns a young schoolteacher to the inner-city high school from which he graduated, to minister to a remedial class of streetwise outcasts called the "sweathogs."

None of these shows achieved the overwhelming ratings success enjoyed by *M*A*S*H* or even *The Mary Tyler Moore Show*, but their audiences were substantial and steady, and this, together with the critical acclaim many earned and the Emmies they carried off year after year, persuaded the networks to let them run long after others had been cut from the schedules. In each case the central group of characters works in a relatively low-status occupation "just for the time being." Almost all are salaried employees in organizational settings. Most dream (like their viewers, perhaps) of having other, more glamorous careers in writing, acting, singing, or sports. And of course "for the time being" usually means forever, with the work-family nurturing and sustaining the hopes of more fulfilling work, consoling its members when their dreams fail to materialize, and providing the emotional sustenance they can no longer expect from outside. One or two realize their dreams: *Barney Miller*'s Harris writes a successful police novel (though he subsequently develops writer's block); *Taxi*'s Bobby finds acting work in Hollywood but returns to visit his old friends, and in this way the dream of success and upward mobility is kept alive.

In time, too, these work groups take on an ethnic diversity that builds on the acceptance of personal idiosyncrasy and cultural difference, extending the affirmative vision of harmonious pluralism with Jews, blacks, and Hispanics each maintaining their separate identities within the binding frame of the great family of America. Whereas the domestic comedies of Norman Lear raise questions of race and ethnicity and render them problematic, the workplace comedies of the 1970s both express ethnic pride and resolve racial tension by harmonizing difference within a single community.

The image of family is at its most potent in the workplace comedy, organizing the progression of plot, gathering in characters, and shaping their relationships to one another. The hour-long episodic series, especially the police and detective shows, rely more heavily on action, event, and denouement. Drama, I argued in Chapter 2, requires the telling of a story, a stronger moral tone, heroes and villains confronting good and evil, and the narrative closure of winners and losers. Still, as the boundaries between comedy and dramatic series grow more blurred, the family metaphor comes more and more to shape the workplace dramatic series as well as the comedies. In part this is because the television professionals of the 1970s are predominantly salaried employees in organizational settings rather than lone entrepreneurs. Typically the workplace drama focuses on the daily life of a small department in a large institution, whether newspaper, hospital, or law-enforcement agency, lending itself to the ensemble of characters seen in the situation comedy and drawing the domesticity of the sitcom into the public sphere.

The crime series, which had dwindled to a trickle during the 1960s, returned in full force in the 1970s. In almost every season the top twenty shows boasted at least four crime dramas, the majority of which were police rather than detective shows. NBC's *Sunday Mystery Movie*, for example, aired four crime dramas (*Columbo, McCloud, McMillan and Wife,* and *Quincy*) in weekly rotation. All were about police in West Coast cities or New York (Quincy was a forensic pathologist employed in the Los Angeles Police Department), and all were popular enough to join favorites such as *Kojak* and *Hawaii Five-O* as weekly series.

To some degree the crime shows of the 1970s retain the ingredients inherited from the movies and reshaped by television in the 1950s, namely, the repeated rehearsal of toned-down violent action and event, the clear narrative progression in which law and justice triumph over evil and chaos, and the sharp lines drawn between good and evil, heroism and villainy. The police of the 1950s crime show had been drab and scrupulously law-abiding in contrast with the sparkling glamor and social marginality of the more ubiquitous private investigator. In the 1970s the policeman becomes not glamorous but more sophisticated, streetwise, and colorful, while the less numerous private detectives (perspiring, rotund Cannon with his epicurean tastes; shambling, wry Jim Rockford—only Mannix retains the high-living urbanity of earlier private eyes) parody their earlier image.

The regular viewer who is familiar with the genre's predictable conventions knows not only what is going to happen and who will win but when victory will occur in the sixty-minute cycle. The difference between shows comes to rest with the particularities of the hero's character and style: Kojak's lollipops, his brutal panache, and his breathy, animal sentimentality; Columbo's crumpled raincoat and head-scratching, apologetic revelations; McCloud's cowboy-in-New-York innocence. The quirkiness of the central character, together with his more ironic sense of corruption within the agencies of law enforcement as well as on the streets, allows the modern crime show to mix drama and comedy in ways that approach the conventions of the sitcom. The cop show further overlaps with the workplace comedy as it comes to emphasize the police hero's reliance on close personal relations with his peers. Kojak does battle with criminals *and* with district attorneys from the home base of his department. If his relations with Detectives McNeil, Crocker, and Stavros are more segmented than the all-embracing interdependence of the professional group in *Barney Miller,* they begin nevertheless to acquire the same exclusive intimacy. A similar progression is evident in the medical drama. The older-younger physician duo established in the 1960s is sustained in *Marcus Welby, M.D.* in the early 1970s but other medical shows, such as *Medical Center* and *Trapper John, M.D.*, relocate the pair within a hospital work group that comes to define their private as well as professional lives.

Not surprisingly, one of the fullest realizations of the work-family in a dramatic series comes from MTM Productions. *Lou Grant* spins off Mary Richards's crotchety boss into his own series as editor of the city desk at the *Los Angeles Tribune,* a family-owned daily newspaper undergoing modernization. More a docudrama than a melodrama, the series strives conscientiously for realism, paying painstaking attention to the details of everyday journalistic life. It is also self-consciously "relevant" in its subject matter, structuring weekly stories around current social and political issues such as rape, environmental pollution, exploitation of migrant workers and illegal aliens, and corruption in big business. What gives the show its dramatic bite, however, is not just the topicality of its concerns, nor even the integration of "issues" into daily life at the *Tribune,* but the responses and actions of the characters, separately and together, to whom the viewer becomes attached over time. The deepening ties between the *Tribune*'s city desk reporters provide a quieter, slice-of-life relevance that pulls in the viewer to their emotional as well as occupational concerns.

Lou continues to grow from the more traditional, gruff paterfamilias with a heart of gold that he was in the early days of *The Mary Tyler Moore Show* into a richer and more complex figure; he is still the tough, acid-tongued pro, but he becomes more introspective, principled, and democratic as the series unfolds. Mrs. Pynchon, the feisty publisher of the *Tribune,* receives the deference owed a matriarchal dowager, but it is Lou (and, more marginally, the stolid managing editor, Charlie Hume) who commands the loyalty and respect of junior reporters Billie, Rossi, and Donovan; it is Lou who adjudicates their rivalries and disputes, praises their achievements, and consoles them in failure or defeat.

A young black reporter is raped, and the normally oblivious Rossi treats her with a brotherly sympathy and sensitivity that survives her denial, anger, and depression and extends to having her stay in his apartment until she recovers. The rape also resurrects old ghosts for Donovan's current girlfriend, herself a past victim of rape, and forces Donovan to confront the complexity of his own feelings about associating with a rape victim. Again and again the junior reporters become personally involved with each other and with the people they write about. "Animal," the photographer, becomes obsessed with the beautiful face of a young girl whose drowning he accidentally witnessed and captured with his camera; Lou must talk him out of his obsession and sustain him through his disillusionment as the truth about her emotional instability emerges. Billie finds herself unable to maintain an appropriate professional distance when she researches a story on the drug DES and its side effects since she herself was a DES baby; she turns to Mrs. Pynchon for support. Rossi becomes attached to a "sociopathic" young woman facing execution. Rossi and Billie bicker and compete over stories. But it is the capacity of the group for mutual loyalty and sustenance and the power of the elders to teach and sustain their younger colleagues that establish the show's rhythm and give it continuity. Their life together can redeem or compensate for the shocks and vicissitudes of modern urban life and provide certainty in an uncertain world.[6]

The striking feature, then, of television comedy and dramatic series with workplace settings is that they almost invariably serve as sites for the development of primary relationships of solidarity, authority, and subordination more commonly associated with families than with secondary occupational groupings. In an age when workplaces are typically large, rationalized, and streamlined, the television workplace is a haven within a harsh and unprepossessing institutional world—cozy, even ramshackle, but above all lived-in, strewn with cherished personal articles. The authority figure is still in every case male, but it is a progressive and androgynous rather than autocratic patriarchy. Barney Miller is authoritative but also nurturant, shielding his junior officers from the demands and arbitrary hurts of the outside world as well as from their own adolescent blunders. *M*A*S*H*'s Colonel Potter administers army rules with a flexibility that allows him to bend or ignore them if they compromise the welfare of the 4077th or the humanitarian treatment of war casualties. Alex Rieger in *Taxi* combines supportive concern with an unobtrusive authority that is neatly set off by Louie, the diminutive dispatcher whose blustery efforts at dictatorship command neither liking nor respect from the rank-and-file cabdrivers. Bob Hartley in *The Bob Newhart Show* and Arthur Carlson in *WKRP in Cincinnati* offer an asexual, tolerant benevolence that is more maternal than patriarchal. In contrast with the more matriarchal domestic comedy, mothers are conspicuous by their virtual absence from the television workplace. Despite their womanly softness and nurturant qualities, Billie in *Lou Grant*, Mary Richards, Elaine Nardo in *Taxi*, and *WKRP*'s luscious Jennifer all have more the character of cherished daughters, spunky and achieving but girlish and vulnerable, than they do of mothers ruling their families. The television workplace may speak to the concerns of the large number of women entering the labor force in the postwar period, but authority remains a male preserve; the implication is that television feminism has its limits.

The family atmosphere of these work groups is lent power and structure and sealed off by the virtual confinement of lasting emotional ties within the work group. Few characters have durable outside relationships, let alone stable marriages. In *Lou Grant* only Charlie Hume is a married man. Mrs. Pynchon is a widow whose chief companion outside work is a dog. Lou is divorced and never remarries. Rossi, Donovan, and Animal all remain steadfastly single and live alone, making only transient attachments for the most part. Billie eventually marries Ted, a basketball player, but subsequent episodes remain almost empty of allusions to her married state or the changes it might generate in her work life. "Rossi knows things about me that even Ted doesn't know!" she remarks in a barroom conversation with her colleagues. The same is true in *Barney Miller* and *Taxi*. Even Barney's apparently unassailable marriage shows signs of foundering in later episodes. Alex Rieger has been divorced for twenty years, and Elaine is a single parent. The police hero is unencumbered but no longer has to be a widower; he (and occasionally she) can be divorced or simply unattached. Doctors continue for the most part to be widowers, although Trapper John is divorced, and his former wife makes occasional appearances on the show.

The essential ingredients of private life are to be found in the workplace; but unlike in soap operas, where love affairs between coworkers wax and wane as a matter of routine, the emotional bonds in prime-time workplace shows are sibling ties and bonds between parents and children. The incest taboo operates here, as do its countervailing forces of mutual attraction: Billie and Donovan occasionally refer to their past relationship; Lou and Mary hover around romance; Alex and Elaine decamp to Paris for a whirlwind affair that they cannot maintain when they return home. Taboos and desires are sustained in uneasy but tantalizing contradiction. The unpalatable fragility of family and other emotional life is presented implicitly, pushed out to the fringes, and redeemed by the close, supportive ties of the work-family.

The "children" squabble and compete, scoring off each other and vying for the attention of their leader-parent, whom they struggle to be like while they simultaneously rebel against his authority. The authority figure is almost always middle-aged, but often a show has its "elders," such as *Barney Miller*'s garrulous Inspector Luger, who has nothing to do and strains Barney's infinite patience to the breaking point by carting him off for irrelevant private conferences conducted in stagy whispers. Fish, the show's grandfather figure, is plagued by mysterious afflictions and exudes a weary fatalism; he is perpetually on the verge of retirement. In one episode he wanders off and arrives late at the office, only to inform a distraught Barney that he is "practicing to see what it's like not coming to work every day."

Thus in the 1970s the pragmatic and internal industrial reasons for the growing salience of the workplace and imagery of professionalism in the television narrative reach deeper into significant areas of cultural change. Cultural criticism and other kinds of popular narrative during this period suggest that the professional group comes to rival, even replace, the family as a focus of longing for primary group identity. With families perceived as deeply troubled, the hopes and fantasies of a sustaining community turn to work relations and professional allegiances. This is not to suggest that the "real" workplace is free from conflict, merely that in this period the family becomes the most visible source of tension. In television, as I argued in Chapter 2, the familial structure of the workplace had begun to take shape in the 1950s with Westerns and police dramas and became stronger as the continuity of the episodic series subordinated plot to character development. In the 1970s the television work-family maps a new social field in which it serves as the "inside" shielding the individual from a threatening outside world that includes the troubled home-family.

It may be that the television workplace, which by virtue of its relative unfamiliarity to viewers is ripe for fantasy, fulfills desires on more than one level. It caters to the wish for a family that, unlike many if not most contemporary families, provides normative markers for living through the exercise of a firm but gentle and democratic authority, and at the same time it serves as a haven from the outside world, indeed a base from which to conquer, avenge, or reduce the impersonal forces of that world. By building a small and intimate place within the work organization, the television narrative also satisfies the desire for workplaces whose cultures more closely resemble those of tolerant, egalitarian families or communities and thus fulfill the yearning for community within the professional group.

In the imagery of prime-time television, as in the occupational world, the terms *profession* and *professionalism* have come to embrace a range of shifting meanings. In its most limited sense professionalism has to do with ideas about occupational skills, services, and autonomy; but here the term achieves almost infinite elasticity since nearly all television occupations are portrayed as professions in one way or another. Television history has seen a steady expansion in the occupational horizons of prime time. Chapter 2 reviewed the transition from shows about the police and private investigators, the professional cowboys of the 1950s, through the medical and legal shows of the 1960s. In the 1970s the continuing preoccupation with medicine and the return of law-enforcement dramas are accompanied by a shift to middle-range occupations, as in the media shows of MTM Productions, as well as lower-echelon police work.

In all these shows the appeal of professionals derives less from their formal training, knowledge, or skills than from their commitment, their integrity of character, and their moral and cultural authority. From policemen to journalists to physicians, all are immersed in a passionate and total commitment to their jobs and their publics. Few if any television professionals care about wealth or status. As in the work dramas of previous decades, money is scarcely mentioned except by villains or other negative figures. Service, which is usually defined by healing, defending, or educative activities, is a primary ethical value. The *M*A*S*H* physicians engage viewers not just because they are surgeons, nor even because they possess specialized scientific knowledge. Viewers are invited to identify with their characters, which, individually and collectively, are kindly, compassionate, loyal, and tolerant; with their absolute commitment to healing, no matter whether the patient is friend or foe in the war; and with their guidance in matters of individual development and public morality.

This understanding of the meaning of professionalism is clearly inspired by the ideology of the so-called free professions and is a curious application, given that by the mid-1970s there remain few self-employed practitioners depicted in television entertainment. Almost all are salaried employees, the majority in large organizations. Since *Marcus Welby, M.D.* none of the successful medical shows have been about doctors in private practice.[7] In law enforcement, police precincts outnumber the offices of private investigators. The media shows of MTM Productions all have organizational settings. Only Bob Hartley, a clinical psychologist, is in private practice, but his office is located in a building housing other medical professionals.

The transition is significant. As the television professionals make their move from autonomy to dependence on a remote administrative authority, their conflicts shift into a different register. The discussion of the television professional in Chapter 2 suggested that the function of the television lawman in the 1950s was largely integrative, smoothing the path of social change, reconciling and harmonizing the relations between the individual, the group, and a fundamentally benevolent society. Even the private detective's breezy disregard for due process carried no implication of the *essential* evil of legal institutions. Evil was primarily invested in the insane or amoral deviant. Similarly, in the 1960s Ben Casey and Dr. Kildare pitted their skills against disease and human folly or ignorance, for the most part under the auspices of kindly superiors and hospital administrators. They were part of the system, and the system functioned on behalf of the people. In the 1970s a new enemy appears—the organization itself—and the hero (occasionally the heroine) engages in battle within its walls. The boundaries of power and authority break up and regroup into new alignments in which contrasting meanings of professionalism play a central role.

The contradictions facing salaried employees who also perceive themselves as professionals are addressed most explicitly and conventionally in shows that aim self-consciously at "realistic" portrayals of modern occupational life. In *The Mary Tyler Moore Show* a newswriters' strike splits not only the station but the WJM family down the middle. Mary is acutely distressed because, as management, she and Lou must cross the picket line and continue working, even though her sympathies lie with Murray and the other striking workers. She confides her misery to Rhoda, who is unsympathetic: "You're the first management person anyone in my family has socialized with . . . I come from a long line of labor people," and she adds encouragingly, "Life isn't easy when you're a dirty rotten scab!" Ted, by contrast, is aghast when his own union branch, the artists and performers, joins the strike: "I'm an individualist . . . the union's never done anything for me!" Mary and Lou proceed to tie themselves in knots trying to bring out the news alone. Lou, fortifying himself from the stock of liquor he keeps in his desk, gets very drunk but manages to read the news on the air perfectly. "You're so professional," coos an admiring Mary on his return; then, as he disappears into his office, she asks, "Where are you going?" Lou, heading for the booze, tells her, "I'm going to get a little more professional"—a sly comment on the convenient elasticity of modern definitions of professionalism. Murray and Gordie sit in a bar convulsed with laughter at the inept efforts of management to do their jobs. Ted, true to his fickle, unaffiliated self, tries to enlist support for a petition that the union accept management's offer. The strike is settled with few gains for the workers. If viewers' sympathies are clearly engaged with the strikers, they are also mobilized for employees who find themselves caught between management and labor. Resolution is achieved only in the internal solidarity of the work-family, which functions as a buffer against the unfeeling organization.

In *WKRP in Cincinnati* the radio station's hard-pressed titular head, Mr. Carlson, refuses to give his staff their Christmas bonus. "This here's a business, y'know!" he blusters, trying to get tough. "Last year you said it was a family!" protests Venus Flytrap, the black disc jockey. "Yes, well," huffs the discomfited boss, "it's a *family* business!" Similar dilemmas emerge in *Lou Grant*. Mrs. Pynchon expresses concern over the leaking of a confidential salary list. In her view it is poor professional etiquette to disclose what people earn. In fact, she implies, it is inappropriate to discuss money at all, since the *Tribune* is a loyal and happy family enterprise. When it is revealed that women on the paper earn less than men, the basis for her concern shifts, and she "hopes this is not discrimination." Her deputy, Charlie Hume, assures her that "it just takes time to catch up," to which the testy dowager replies, "Well, they understand that, don't they?" But Lou must protect the interests of his brood as employees, not the faithful organization men of the family firm Mrs. Pynchon inherited from her husband. He confronts her directly: "Would *you* understand?" As the series develops, Lou finds himself increasingly caught between management and labor, professional and administrative norms, technological progress and worker rights, traditional paternalism and a more egalitarian, universalistic authority.

In the studiously evenhanded documentary style of *Lou Grant* such problems are depicted as structural; struggles emerge out of rationally expressed conflicts of interest and only become personal in a secondary way. In the police and medical shows, in which drama rather than authenticity is of the essence, the issues translate into good and bad characters, heroes and villains. Kojak is forever pitting his practical humanism against bureaucratic, insensitive district attorneys. "Sure I stretch the law sometimes," he admonishes an ambitious young D.A., "Maybe it needs stretching a little! Get back into the streets, baby!" As a medical examiner, Quincy is accountable to both medical and legal establishments, whose stuffy adherence to procedure inspires him to impassioned speeches about truth and justice. Humanity encounters officialdom; flexibility confronts enslavement to protocol.

Comedy, as seen in the domestic shows, is a potent vehicle for the expression of ambivalence and opposition because it can render its targets absurd, impotent, or idiotic as well as immoral or insane. In *M*A*S*H* hostility toward the army administrative apparatus is a recurring theme. Colonel Potter remarks of a visiting administrator, "His I.Q. is lower than his boot size, but the army had enough savvy to put him in a job where he couldn't do any harm. They made him a general in medical administration." This view is readily endorsed by Klinger: "Those who can't, manage those who can!" Such devices accomplish the symbolic reduction of the feared enemy's power, a revenge no less satisfying for being confined to the imaginary sphere. In *Barney Miller* such strategies form the thematic backbone of the narrative. Bureaucrats, whether inside or outside the organization, are routinely presented in a negative light as silly, unpleasant, or insidious people. The regular "bad guy" of the show is the weaselly, probing Lieutenant Scanlon from Internal Affairs—despised and invariably outwitted in his efforts to catch Barney and his charges in some infringement of police regulations. Again and again the narrative is pushed along by a parade of sententious, incompetent, or spaced-out public officials and corporate executives, powerful adversaries to be ridiculed or outmaneuvered. A federal official from the Bureau of Indian Affairs announces with unctuous dignity, "I deal with entire nations, not people!" When Barney asks a stockbroker accused of stealing from his own colleague whether he has any friends, the man replies, "I told you . . . I'm a stockbroker!"

The expression of populist animus toward the rich and the powerful is central in *Barney Miller*. Barney and his colleagues habitually play Robin Hood and his merrie men. They overcome nasty or ridiculous bureaucrats or corporate fat cats and redistribute their power and resources to the common people, represented by a procession of small shopkeepers, timid, spinsterish librarians, brassy hookers, and social misfits (all played by the same group of rotating actors, which enhances their homogeneity), who wander through the twelfth precinct as plaintiffs, detainees, or garrulous nuisances. In one episode a multinational development corporation presses charges against a humble delicatessen owner for his long-standing habit of walking to work across their newly acquired property. Sergeant Dietrich carries out some speedy legal research on his own initiative and unearths a long-forgotten easement statute, enabling the short, rotund shopkeeper to turn the tables and file a complaint against his accusers (represented by a very tall, besuited lawyer). The little man cheerfully resists all attempts to buy him off and, accepting Dietrich's deft sleight of hand, decides to press charges—"if it's not too much trouble!"

If public officials and businessmen serve as targets for ambivalence or open resentment, so too do certain kinds of professionals. Doctors and lawyers, far from the godlike figures of earlier decades, are often indistinguishable from administrators and executives in their capacity for unbridled self-interest, bumbling incompetence, or detachment from the reality of everyday contingency and individual difference. In the medical dramas, for example, a split between "good" and "bad" physicians is often set up. Testifying for the defense in a courtroom battle, Quincy comments to his faithful assistant Sam about a freelance forensic scientist hired by the prosecution to testify, "He won't lie, but I've seen him bend the truth like a willow!" while a colleague remarks to Quincy with a mixture of admiration and scorn, "I think you're a nice, bright fellow who's got his head stuck in a bucket full of compassion." The viewer is clearly being invited to identify with the compassionate Quincy.

This sense of division *within* the ranks of the organization is strong stuff compared to the unruffled togetherness of the medical world in *Dr. Kildare* or *Ben Casey,* most of whose characters speak in the medical *we*. But it is mild indeed compared with the contempt heaped on the medical profession in comedy. *Barney Miller's* Sergeant Harris, who is worried about impending layoffs in the police precinct, sighs wistfully, "I should've been a doctor. When people call you on the phone in the middle of the night and say, 'Hey man, I'm in trouble, can you help me?' you get to say no, and hang up!" Lawyers too are regularly lampooned or treated with mistrust and dislike. A police careerist introduces himself proudly at the precinct as a policeman "and now a lawyer," earning from Harris a curled lip and the response "Oh! I like you already!"

The character of Dietrich supplies a walking satirical commentary on medical and legal expertise. Formerly a medical *and* a law student, he is always ready with a handy quote from the latest research. "Studies show . . . ," "We now know that . . ." he solemnly intones, but his lecture is delivered to his exasperated colleagues in a textbook monotone interrupted by a disclaiming grin that clearly announces how much he enjoys both the satire and the irritation it causes his colleagues. The precinct is plagued with a flurry of anonymous false alarms, and Dietrich speculates on the causes: "It could be a schizophrenic acting out his fantasies, an individual rebelling against the authority of society . . ."; but he is interrupted by the more prosaic Wojo: ". . . or a cheeseburger waiting to take a potshot at a cop!" Psychiatrists are attacked with particular savagery. When a humorless police psychiatrist insists on subjecting the entire squad to a battery of Rorschach tests, Barney explodes, "To each his own! That's the name of *that* test!" while Detective Yamana subverts in merrier fashion by earnestly declaring to the uneasy psychiatrist that he sees only an elephant lying on his back with a hat on.

In series with domestic settings, as I showed in Chapter 4, similar themes of resentment abound, particularly with regard to doctors and psychological professionals. But the television family has fewer resources for resistance. In *One Day at a Time* Ann Romano can fire off as much vitriol as she likes about the unavailability or incompetence of doctors; she has little choice but to take the help that is provided. Rhoda has decidedly mixed feelings about her manipulative marriage counselor, but she depends on him and even allows him to wheedle her into a date. The domestic television family has few choices; it can either place itself in the hands of outside experts, or convert itself into a therapeutic agency by internalizing the language and functions of those institutions. In *Family* the Lawrences have their own built-in honest lawyer in Doug, and Kate's psychological language and "insights" turn her into a de facto family therapist.

By contrast, the television workplace becomes the site for more successful struggles for autonomy. The antagonisms and conflicts that are repeatedly acted out serve to construct a dualistic world in which "good" and "bad" professionals are played off against each other. The differences are partly characterological—"bad" professionals appear variously as childish, egocentric, stupid, pompous, or sinister—and partly moral—such people are often deceitful, ruthless, indifferent to suffering, rigid yet arbitrary in the exercise of authority. These dichotomies of character and ethics shade off into a broader imagery of the bases of institutional power in modern life. It is a vision of power grown more menacing than the kindly authority of doctors Kildare, Casey, and Welby. In the shows of the 1970s power derives from an expertise based on formal principles and abstract intellectual knowledge and the use of complex technologies remote from the concerns of ordinary people.[8] Hence the incompetence, the irrelevant babbling of textbook jargon, and the dumb helplessness before the practical exigencies of everyday life.

In part this hostility to formal expertise reflects the robust strain of anti-intellectualism that has long permeated American popular culture. At least two episodes of *The Mary Tyler Moore Show* lambasted television critics, respectively portrayed as an unscrupulous yellow journalist and a puffed-up intellectual snob. "You creep!" screams the usually placid Mary when the latter uses his nightly spot on the news to trash the very show on which he appears, "What show did you ever produce? Have you no sense of proportion? Attacking the individuals and producers of a tiny TV station, who're doing the best they can!" The hapless protector of cultural standards receives that tried and true missile of the people, a pie in the face. This may be read as a personal message from the show's creators to critics, but it also offers a broader comment on the cultural establishment that designates television as junk and its creators and audiences as philistines.

The dichotomy also serves in the construction of a more populist and humanized version of professionalism. The "people's professional" is personified in modest organizational heroes like Barney Miller, Lou Grant, Alex Rieger, and Bob Hartley. In *The Mary Tyler Moore Show* Mary asks Lou to give a guest lecture at her evening class in journalism. His speech is brief: "Good newswriting is getting the facts, getting them fast and presenting them well." A student hastily tries to fill the stunned silence that follows with a question about appropriate books to read. "Books?" snaps Lou, "Forget books! You don't learn from books!" Bob Hartley explains to his substitute, an academic psychologist whose abstract approach with Bob's therapy group has ended in disaster, "You lectured them instead of listening to them. This isn't a classroom, this is real life!"

What gives these figures their appeal and authority is a sense of substantive rather than formal knowledge, skills, and ethics; the application of commonsense solutions to everyday problems; a liberal emphasis on civil rights flexibly administered; and a pluralist tolerance for ethnic diversity and personal idiosyncrasy. Above all, they are absolutely committed to the protection of the average citizen, not so much from criminals, hucksters, or lunatics, but precisely from the clutches of those who hold impersonal power—the "abstract" professionals, public officials, and business executives. This is a far cry from the conformism of Joe Friday, Matt Dillon, or Marcus Welby. In this way, too, the difficulties of retaining pluralist liberal values in a society in which power is unequally distributed are glossed over or resolved within the narrative.

The strength of the aggression expressed toward "abstract" professionals suggests also a measure of dependency, awe, and fear. When Harris (*Barney Miller*) wishes sardonically that he were a doctor, he is calling attention to the inordinate power of the medical profession, but he also envies the security of doctors and the freedom they have to do as they please. A similar ambivalence emerges in *The Bob Newhart Show;* Bob feels professionally slighted when his neighbor Howard turns to Bob's wife Emily for advice about how to cope with his unruly son. Miffed, Bob rebukes them stuffily, "After all, I *am* a psychologist!" to which his wife, an elementary-school teacher, replies with wicked glee, "Well, Bob, I think that's what's wrong with this country . . . people going to a specialist for a job they could do themselves!" And she turns to counsel Howard—in the full-blown psychotherapeutic rhetoric Bob sometimes uses with his group. Bob endorses and parodies the psychological mode by turns; indeed his quality of hesitating ambivalence is a hallmark of fine MTM scriptwriting.

In the writing of many shows it has become common practice to consult experts, legitimizing the very expertise that has come under fire in those same shows. Networks routinely submit the scripts of medical series to the American Medical Association for vetting and approval. Every *Lou Grant* episode was read for "authenticity" by a journalist from the *Los Angeles Times*. Indeed the show is intended to inform viewers about the practice of journalism. The occupational ideology of newsmaking—objectivity, neutrality, responsibility to the public—is explicitly endorsed: "If I were interested in money," says Billie, "I wouldn't be a reporter"; "I may step on some toes," Rossi admits, "but all I really care about is the story"; and Charlie Hume declares, "We just report the news. We don't make it." Again and again in dramatic series the manifest message legitimizes and defers to the superior knowledge of accredited experts, while antagonism makes itself felt at more implicit levels of the narrative. By contrast, in comedy it is the hostility that most often lies uppermost.

The dualism between benign and malevolent professionalism, and substantive and formal knowledge, may serve more broadly as a metaphor for antimodern impulses in American culture. In a society based on centralized institutional power the television workplace expresses local autonomy. In the midst of the large, anonymous city it creates family and community. Where managerial and technical controls have imposed a rigid homogeneity, television celebrates diversity, human initiative, and tolerance of individual and group differences. The contemporary television hero, the "people's professional," counters the paralyzing incursions of formal, especially therapeutic, expertise with native wit, commonsense practicality, and ordinary decency.

The television world of work, in sum, is primarily a world of relationship and emotionality—of community. In this sense it extends and comments on, rather than departs from, the domestic series. The television workplace has come to resound with themes that speak to contemporary anxiety and desire, and it appears to provide a more plausible symbolic "place" in which to resolve these than the domestic sphere. The emotional heart of the workplace series is not work activity, not even the star, but the relationships between colleagues whose own family attachments have become either severely attenuated or nonexistent. The medical team in *M*A*S*H*, the television producers of WJM in the *The Mary Tyler Moore Show*, the detectives of the twelfth precinct in *Barney Miller*—all these groups display both the claustrophobic testiness and the warm solidarity many of us carry around as family ideals in our heads. "You've been a family to me," cries a tearful Mary

Richards when WJM is shut down at the end of the show's seventh season. If the television workplace offers a community that compensates for the ravaged instability of the domestic shows, it may also suggest to a career-oriented generation that the opportunities for emotional engagement and support no longer lie in the family but in the workplace. And the profound sense of confusion about the boundaries dividing public and private life documented by cultural critics may be what allows the television workplace to replace and compensate for the domestic arena with such plausibility.

6

Family Television
Then and Now

This book began as a recovery of the imagery of family produced by American network television series in the 1970s. I was interested in the light that symbolic representation in popular culture could shed on the changing social psychology of American family life in a period when family issues were being defined as both significant and troubling. Accordingly, I was comparing the television narrative not only with its own past and that of other popular cultural forms but also with other kinds of cultural interpretation, notably the work of critics and social scientists interested in the relationships between family and public life.

As the work unfolded, the empirical questions I was asking about television's changing imagery of family and workplace compelled me to ask the kinds of theoretical and methodological questions that are being raised in a lively debate among students of culture and the media on both sides of the Atlantic—questions about how the television industry works, about the nature of the particular interpretive modes of television, and about its relationship to other kinds of discourse including those of lived experience.

The first set of questions concerns the relationship between different forms of cultural interpretation. On what basis can one make comparisons and distinctions between different kinds of interpretive work, whether in television or other kinds of popular culture, cultural criticism, or the ongoing interpretive activity of everyday life? A second, related set of questions concerns the study of the particular language of television. What does it mean to conceive of television as a text *producing* meanings? How are the narratives of television shaped by the industry's characteristic practices of production and reception? How does the particular language of television work on the viewer, and how do viewers interact with television? Are there significant differences between the readings of television produced by "naive" viewers and those produced by "expert" viewers subjecting television to self-conscious critical scrutiny? How does television participate or intervene in the everyday lives of viewers? I have tried to address these issues by attending to television not in the terms of an analysis of its "content" or "effects" on viewers but as a constellation of social practices of production and reception, which become embedded in the shifting meanings of the narrative.

In Chapter 1 I argued that both television and cultural criticism in the 1970s revealed common themes that identified the American family as a major source of conflict and anxiety about social change. I suggested that both addressed a mounting sense of confusion about the changing boundaries between family and work, private and public spheres, and the implications of these changes for community life, and that television reworked and commented on the public concerns voiced by cultural critics, social scientists, and policymakers within the frame of its own language, raising and then symbolically resolving the troubling issues of its time and place.

Chapter 2 began to uncover the workings of that language by offering a structural, organizational, and historical account of the growth of the most powerful television genre, the episodic series, which served as a frame for the development of a specifically televisual articulation of family and workplace. The domesticity that came to define the series form in the first two decades of network television was grounded not just in the resonance of an idealized family for viewers steeped in postwar values of progress, affluence, and national consensus, which were to be achieved through the integrative power of the domestic unit, but also in the emergent political economy of the television industry itself. In the networks' first two decades they searched for an undifferentiated, predictable mass audience of regular viewers for programs and commercials that would sustain the advertising revenues on which they were so dependent. This search helped to create that formulaic mix of repetition and continuity that was to define the episodic series and fashion an image of family so benign and uncontroversial, so broadly middle-class and free of ethnic partisanship, indeed so free of ethnicity in general—that it would offend no one. And just as the doctrine of "least objectionable programming" created consensual, idealized families, so it helped tame the early dramatic series inherited from film by turning the television workplace into a domestic allegory that served to integrate the individual and the primary group into a just and benevolent social order, with the professional hero at its center.

Thus the shaping of genre, form, and meaning in television entertainment has rested as much on the routine practices of the network television industry as on the aesthetic conventions television inherited from theater, film, and radio, or on the ideological climate of time and place. Studying the mechanics of *how* television routinely creates its images teaches us how dominant ideas are reproduced and modified by people who seek merely to sell packages of entertainment or, as network executives frequently (if disingenuously) protest, give the public what it wants. In Chapter 3 this relationship between the work of producers, the images they create, and the constructions of their audiences was explored at a critical juncture in the history of the television entertainment industry, when changes in network orthodoxies about ratings strategies created a climate of lively innovation in prime-time programming. The search by executives and independent producers for themes that would engage the attention of more specialized viewers within the mass audience—younger, more educated urban consumers whose willingness to spend made them attractive to advertisers—facilitated a break with the consensual tone of television in the 1950s and 1960s, allowing the turbulence of the social movements of the 1960s to become encoded into the television series in the form of "relevant" programming. In this way social issues whose importance had already been ratified by the news media and other wings of the "information industry" became legitimate topics for entertainment programming.

Chapters 4 and 5 examined how the narratives of episodic series escaped from the shaping hands of producers and scheduling executives to become objectified as "relevant" tales of family and work that spoke to deeper, more diffuse anxieties lying beneath the neat packaging of "media consciousness." In the 1950s and 1960s the television sitcom had generated a monolithic family imagery congruent with the commercial exigencies of mass-market television, but one that also endorsed the "middle classlessness" of postwar ideology, proposing the nuclear family as the friendly broker between the individual and wider social institutions, both economic and normative. In the 1970s that consensus fell apart on screen, prompted at the industrial level by a more pluralistic and specialized vision of the television audience, but also reflecting a political and social collapse that had begun in the mid-1960s. Once a cozy nest embedded in a kindly institutional world, the television family became a seething locus of anger and fear, not only about rapid and bewildering changes in the outside world, but also about its own integrity and survival. Yet the longing for a solidary primary community persisted in an idealized workplace that offered not only a redeeming family but also an alternative vision of professional community to the decaying dream of corporate life—a haven in a heartless world. To find that haven in, of all places, the large organization (a source of remote but invasive domination in the lives of many American workers, according to the cultural critics of the period) is at first puzzling. But if we understand the television narrative as a *commentary* on, and *resolution* of, our troubles rather than a reflection of the real conditions of our lives, it becomes possible to read the television work-family as a critique of the alienating modern corporate world and an affirmation of the possibility of community and cooperation amid the loose and fragmentary ties of association. That affirmation draws for its sustenance not only on the deferred pain of much contemporary family life but also on a long-standing desire for community and meaning in professional life, lent new significance for emerging generations of career-oriented young people who were coming of age in the more questioning political climate of the 1960s.

In no period, then, does television imagery of family or workplace mirror real conditions of living, though it may, by virtue of its celebration of the ordinary and its mimetic form, appear to do so. In every era I examined, the television narrative addressed prevailing ideas and concerns about family, workplace, and the relationship of both to institutional life and resolved them in particular, recurring ways. The great appeal of all entertainment is its symbolic but satisfying manipulation of desire. In the 1970s television held up for inspection the damage that has been done to family lives, but it gave back whole and satisfying families, displaced into areas where viewers could more comfortably accommodate them.

The changes in meaning were also changes in form. From the 1950s to the late 1970s the episodic series was undergoing a gradual opening out, evident in the continuing shift from situation to character, from tightly structured to looser narratives with more open endings, from harmonious to troubled families, and from an emphasis on the home to a split between home and work. The "relevant" shows also began to move toward greater structural ambiguity as drama and comedy elided into what in the 1980s have come to be called "dramadies"—shows with less explicit story lines, unresolved endings, greater complexity and development of character, and shifting perspectives from one character to the next. The potential always present in comedy for critique, for generating multiple and even dissident voices, was partially freed by commercial considerations that seemed to compel an appeal to more specialized audiences. But as the following discussion of series television in the 1980s suggests, the subversive potential of comedy was to be contained by the simultaneous need to sustain the interest of a broader audience perceived as more mainstream in its values.

The striking feature of series development in the 1980s is the acceleration of these trends and the increased dialogue between the episodic series and other genres in both television and other cultural forms. The boundaries of the series grow more fluid, and some series recombine with other genres; in particular, the series approaches the more ambiguous, unresolved form of the serial. This is particularly true of nighttime soap operas and one-hour dramas such as *Cagney and Lacey, Hill Street Blues,* and *L.A. Law,* as well as *Moonlighting* and *Thirtysomething.* Their multiple story lines, often left unresolved for several weeks, and large families of characters leading chaotic personal lives in which traditional categories of heroism and villainy collapse into a bewildering ambiguity, approximate more closely than ever the conventions of the soap opera, with its shifting perspectives, endless narrative, and motivational uncertainties. Here the "decentering" of the television narrative that began in the character comedies and dramas of the 1970s is pushed even further.

The style of 1980s dramatic series is hip, self-consciously parodic and urbane, gesturing knowingly toward, and plundering from, other television shows, other genres, and other media. One episode of *Moonlighting* recapitulates—and parodies—*The Taming of the Shrew;* another ends with cuts of failed takes, inviting the viewer into the production process and thereby encouraging the viewer to suspend belief in the story's independent reality. *Hill Street Blues* and *L.A. Law* are peppered with arch allusions to pop culture, such as the development of a parodic Captain America–type character over several weeks. An episode of *Cagney and Lacey* harks back to the quiz show scandals of the late 1950s. *Thirtysomething* gives itself over to the depiction of life-style writ large, rendered through a host of cues that signify different decades. Each episode is glued together by period symbols—the low-key guitar music that ushers in the credits, the elliptical references to an undefined collective past ("the sixties") that turns a generation's history into a museum of pop-culture icons. In all these shows comedy tumbles into drama and back again into comedy without warning. Though these patterns are most marked in dramatic series, more and more they are incorporated into comedy series as well; the "girls" of *Designing Women* watch Shere Hite on *The Oprah Winfrey Show* and begin a discussion about "women who hate men." *The Wonder Years*, in which a grown man recalls his life as a twelve-year-old in the summer of 1968, opens with a few bars of "I'll Get By with a Little Help from My Friends" and fades out to the strains of "When a Man Loves a Woman."

This reflexive style is quite self-conscious. It marks the sensibility of a new generation of television writers and producers, including Gary David Goldberg (*Family Ties, Day by Day*), Steven Bochco (*Hill Street Blues, L.A. Law, Hooperman*), Stephen J. Cannell (*The A-Team*), and Michael Mann (*Miami Vice, Crime Story*), whose work seeks to appeal to the younger, more sophisticated generation of viewers who have grown up with television, movies, and rock and roll and can move smoothly between one medium or generic category and the next, aided of course by the ubiquitous reruns. As programming executives turn their marketing attention to even younger viewers—children and teenagers—it is likely that this strain of programming will grow more pronounced in prime-time television, as is evidenced by the emphasis on music video, with its shifting, arcane allusions and chopped-up narratives, and shows like *Miami Vice*, which has the look and feel of a long music video. The growing opportunities for viewers to play around with schedules and commercials and to reshape their own viewing habits with the aid of home video technology add to the fluid intertextuality of much contemporary television. They also threaten to disrupt the disciplinary activity of genre boundaries, pluralizing and relativizing meaning and subverting television's realist claim to mirror a given social world. When the boundaries between genres grow hazier, when comedy and drama interrupt one another, when programs call viewers' attention to the manner of their construction, a naive reading of narrative becomes problematic; the viewer is being schooled in skepticism.

In comedy, too, where the routines of everyday life in the home are rehearsed weekly and the meaning of family picked over and defined, there has been substantial change. In the early seasons of the 1980s the popularity of the domestic comedies seemed to be tapering off and, after Ronald Reagan's massive 1980 victory at the polls, cultural diagnosticians at the networks were confidently announcing a "shift to the right." Initially, as Todd Gitlin (1985) has shown in his interviews with Hollywood producers, they projected from Reagan's victory an interest on the part of viewers in cold-war–style action-adventure series and accordingly created shows like *The CIA* and *Today's FBI*. All were dropped by the end of the 1981 season, which action suggests not only that industry projections were wrong but also that audiences exercise at least the minimal power of not watching.

In fact the shift to the right was expressing itself with greatest force on the domestic front. If in the 1970s the family had been acknowledged as the primary arena for the expression of social conflict, by the early 1980s it had, as Ellen Willis (1982) predicted, become the focus of a fierce backlash led by the religious right. The failure of many states to ratify the Equal Rights Amendment, the struggles over abortion rights and contraception for teenagers, and the call for a return to "basic values" (meaning less government intervention in family matters and a reassertion of parental authority over the young) have all become major issues of public concern. Television, with its earnest scrutiny of other media for cultural trends, has leaped onto the ideological bandwagon not just in news and talk shows but also in its entertainment themes. The made-for-TV movie, with its solemn sociological and therapeutic format, frames most directly the "official" problems of the day—rape, anorexia, mental illness, drug abuse, incest, divorce, homosexuality—and resolves them within the family (Taylor and Walsh 1987).

The top ten shows in the Nielsen ratings for the 1982–1983 season featured only two comedies (*M*A*S*H* and *Three's Company*), and the 1983–1984 season only one (*Kate and Allie*). Critics began writing columns declaring the sitcom dead or dying. But the glittering partnership of NBC's *The Cosby Show* and *Family Ties* in 1984 ensured that it was neither. Once again the formula has changed in the first instance as a response to shifts in industrial practice. The format of these series, which develop discrete themes for small children, teenagers, and adults, for women and men as well as for the family as a whole, suggests a demographics in which several markets are identified and laced together to create a new kind of mass audience (as well, perhaps, as a renewed need to avoid giving offense to viewers). In the exquisite refinement of demographic ratings policies, whole "strips" or evenings of prime time are now designed with particular aggregates of markets in mind, and scheduling becomes a key craft in the networks' race for supremacy.[1] The successful Thursday night lineup that catapulted NBC to the head of the network competition in the mid-1980s began with *Cosby* and *Family Ties*, which secured the mass audience, and after children's bedtime moved smoothly into the adult markets with the work-families of *Cheers*, *Night Court*, and *Hill Street Blues* (later replaced by the glossier *L.A. Law*), in short, an advertiser's paradise.[2] The "strip" of viewing may compel viewers to shift between the subgenres of comedy and dramatic series; but since those categories are now quite blurred within and between shows (given the tendency toward "dramadies," it is unclear whether viewers continue to distinguish between comedies and dramas), that disruption probably registers less with audiences than the continuity of the discourse of family across the series genre and throughout television.

By the middle of the 1980s the sphere of the domestic had reasserted its supremacy in the Nielsen ratings, but with a marked proliferation of family forms. The massive, continuous flow of television, as Hartley (1984) has noted, generates an excess of meanings. Genre rules may in principle function to contain that excess, but when genre boundaries grow hazier and genres plunder each others' forms, the potential for multiple and alternative readings increases. The second half of the decade has seen the single-parent community (*Kate and Allie*), the all-female household (*The Golden Girls, Designing Women*), the all-male household (*Dads, My Two Dads, You Again*), the mixed-race family (*Webster, Diff'rent Strokes, Gimme A Break*), the all-black family (*Amen, 227*), the role-reversed, reconstituted family (*Who's the Boss?*), the self-sufficient family (*Day by Day*, in which a professional couple flees the public sphere altogether by opening a day-care center in their home), and others. From an industrial point of view this pluralism may reflect the mandate of the television producer to place a slightly different spin on the same old formula. But the diversification of family structure also carries the potential for a wide range of interpretations, in particular a more flexible family sensibility. Although family remains the significant frame of both comedy and drama, whether about home or workplace, its meaning changes. The inevitability of nuclear-family life is increasingly called into question, and understandings of family relativized, in a variety of representations of domesticity.

Yet in many series this potential for creating alternative meanings is undercut or diluted by the level of generality, the cheery politics of social adjustment, with which family change is endorsed even in shows that experiment self-consciously with gender and family roles. With few exceptions the family comedies of the 1980s are less genuinely adversarial than those of the early 1970s. "Do I have to be a relative to be family?" a confused little boy asks his mother in *Who's the Boss?* a role-reversal comedy about two single parents (she the breadwinner, he the housekeeper) living together. "Not necessarily," his mother smiles down at him, "a family means people who share each other's lives and care about each other." This may be an unexceptionable definition, given the variety of domestic living arrangements revealed by census data, but it is also virtually meaningless. With the sting of divorce, family poverty, and other problems removed, single parenthood and stepparenting turn into a romp, a permanent pajama party. Even *Kate and Allie*, which began as a witty comedy of divorce manners and a chronicle of the single life encountered the second time around, slipped into the mold of didactic "parenting psychology," focusing more traditionally on children's and teenagers' rites of passage than on adults reinventing normative life. Here the television narrative hedges its bets by nodding in the direction of radical changes in family form and structure without taking them seriously.

Similarly, the vigorous airing of women's concerns observed in the prime-time feminism of the 1970s has been attenuated or transformed. The few attempts to create comedies revolving around single women (including *Mary*, a new vehicle for Mary Tyler Moore) in the first half of the 1980s were quickly cut short when they failed to become immediate ratings successes. In the dramatic series working women abound, but with few exceptions they have become career women, with all the ambivalence that surrounds that trend. In *Cagney and Lacey* both the ambitious Christine Cagney and her partner, the harried working mother Marybeth Lacey, are constantly confronting the conflicts between their police careers and their private lives. In *Thirtysomething* Hope returns to the job she thinks she misses after having a baby—but subsequent episodes virtually ignore her dilemma. Her friend Ellen, a high-powered executive, agonizes frequently about not having the correct maternal or emotional instincts. *The Cosby Show*'s Clair Huxtable, a lawyer, is superwoman incarnate; she embodies a feminine mystique for the 1980s and is rarely seen working or even discussing her work. *Day by Day* plays off its central character, a lawyer who abandons her career to run a day-care center at home with her husband, against a child-hating, narcissistic female stockbroker. The theme of the disillusioned career woman returning home to her suburban family has been featured in more than one late-1980s made-for-TV movie. Thus the celebration of the opening up of women's roles in the 1970s shows becomes, in the 1980s, at best a rehearsal of the costs of careerism for women, at worst an outright reproof for women who seek challenging work. In this way the genuine difficulties women face in reconciling home and work are often casually translated into a backlash against feminism itself.

The true locus of family flux on television in the 1980s may be the nighttime soaps, prime time's closest approximation to the serial. Nothing else on television matches the seething ambiguities and flaring passions of these clans. In one season of *Dynasty* patriarch

Blake Carrington struggles to control, variously, the rivalry between his wife and his former wife; his son Stephen, whose sexual
identity oscillates between homosexual and heterosexual as the plot
requires; his son Adam, who turns out not to be his son at all (so he
adopts him); his niece Leslie, who discovers that her lover was
actually her brother; and his sister Dominique, who, in a grand but
wildly implausible burst of televisual affirmative action, is black. In
season after season the elastic boundaries of the nighttime soaps
expand and contract to admit or expel undiscovered relatives, both
bogus and genuine. It is likely, however, that viewers receive this
subgenre in the high camp spirit in which it is typically offered.
Nighttime soaps declare themselves as florid exaggerations of
reality; no wonder soap stars often collapse into disclaiming giggles
when interviewed on talk shows about the characters they play.

If, as Fiske (1987) has suggested, popular shows are those that
most nearly approximate dominant ideas, then it is to *The Cosby
Show,* whose phenomenal success set a trend for a new wave of
comedies with intact nuclear families, that one must turn to read
those ideas.[3] Like *All in the Family* a decade earlier, *The Cosby
Show* has attracted an enormous amount of attention (most of it
favorable) from critics and public interest groups as well as a vast
and devoted audience; but there the similarity ends. The robustly
working-class Bunker household was never a model of consumer
vitality, nor did it aspire to be. If Archie was dragged by the scruff
of his reluctant neck into the 1970s, the Huxtable family embraces
modernity with enthusiasm. Surrounded by the material evidence
of their success, the Huxtables radiate wealth, health, energy, and
up-to-the-minute style. Indeed *The Cosby Show* offers the same
pleasures as a television commercial—a parade of gleaming
commodities and expensive designer clothing unabashedly enjoyed
by successful professional families. Cosby himself is a gifted
salesman of the goods and services, from Jell-O Pops to E. F.
Hutton, that finance his series.

This conspicuous consumption is a far cry from the relaxed,
unostentatious assumption of material comfort in *Ozzie and Harriet*
or *Father Knows Best*. Some critics have concluded that *The Cosby
Show* and its imitators signify a return to 1950s-style consensual
domestic comedy. Week after week, the show supplies the same
rewards as those offered by family comedy in the 1950s and

1960s—the continuity of orderly lives lived without major trauma or disturbance, stretching back into an identical past and reaching forward into an identical future. But whereas the television families of the 1950s casually took harmony and order for granted, indeed took *the institution of the stable family* for granted, the Huxtables work strenuously and self-consciously at persuading viewers how well they get along. Given the troubled condition of many families in the 1980s, *The Cosby Show* must be palpably compensatory or redemptive for many of its devotees, responding to family distress by articulating the shrill (but reassuringly unambiguous) fundamentalist rhetoric to be found in many areas of private and public life today.

Nothing, in the classical dramatic sense, ever really happens on *The Cosby Show*, which is a virtually plotless chronicle of the small, quotidian details of family life, at whose heart lies a moral etiquette of parenting and a developmental psychology of growing up. Narrative resolution, far tighter than in most domestic comedies since the early 1970s, comes in the form of a learning experience, a lesson in social adjustment for the children. The relentlessly cute Rudy learns to stop bossing her friends around. Theo learns not to embark on expensive projects he has no intention of completing. Sandra and her boyfriend learn to arbitrate their own quarrels over the division of labor. Even Cliff and Clair, despite high-powered careers as physician and lawyer respectively, have all the leisure in the world to spend "quality time" with their offspring, teaching one another parenting by discussion as well as by example. Yet the learning is abstract; in contrast to the families in the character comedies of the 1970s, not one of the Huxtables ever develops. Didacticism is nothing new in network television, but in *The Cosby Show* moral and psychological instruction become monolithic and indisputable. Unlike the Bunkers, for whom every problem became the occasion for an all-out war of ideas, the Huxtables never scream or lose control. True, beneath their beguiling mildness there lurks a casual hostility in which everyone, Mom and Dad included, trades insults and mocks everyone else. But there is no dissent, no real difference of opinion or belief, only vaguely malicious banter that quickly dissolves into sweet agreement—all part of the busy daily manufacture of consensus.

Undercutting the warm color and light and the joking bonhomie is a persistent authoritarianism. The tone is set by Cosby himself, whose prodigious charm overlays a subtle menace: Father knows best, or else. The cuddly, overgrown schoolboy becomes the amused onlooker and then the oracle; he is master of both the strategic silence and the innocent question that lets his children know they have said or done something dumb or gives his wife to understand that her independence is slipping into bossiness. Indeed the impeccable but perfunctory salutes to feminism serve to gloss over the enormous difficulty a woman like Clair might have in juggling her many roles. Behind the democratic gloss of family meetings and the insistence on "communication," Cliff practices a thoroughly contemporary politics of strong leadership, managing conflict with all the skill of a well-trained corporate executive. So too does his lawyer wife, who in one episode during the 1987–1988 season stages a kangaroo court at home for her teenage son Theo, whose crime is not merely arriving home fifteen minutes late but, worse, refusing to tell his parents why. By the end of the show Theo sees the error of his ways.

There is none of the generational warfare that rocked the Bunker household, and this family scarcely needs the openly repressive "tough love" therapy that has cropped up with some regularity in 1980s made-for-TV movies because parental authority has already been internalized. The children put up token displays of playful resistance, then surrender happily to the divine right of parents whose facile knowledge of the difference between right and wrong irons out the inconvenient ambiguities of contemporary life. Since the Huxtables are a supremely intact nuclear family, these ambiguities rarely come up; when they do, though, they occur outside the charmed family circle and remain there. A teenage pregnancy, a drug problem, a worker laid off—occasionally one of the problems that bedevil most families casts a brief shadow on the bright domestic scene and then slinks away, intimidated by the fortress of Huxtable togetherness.

Unlike the sitcoms of the 1950s, whose vision of the social terrain outside the family was as benign as that inside it, and those of the 1970s, which conducted a useful if testy dialogue with public institutions, the world outside *The Cosby Show* appears both diffuse and downright perilous, to the degree that it exists at all. The Huxtables have friends who drift in and out of their lives but no discernible community, indeed no public life to speak of aside from their jobs, which seem to run on automatic pilot. Like Norman Lear's "ethnic comedies" in the 1970s, *The Cosby Show* inhabits a visibly black world, but here its blackness is scarcely alluded to.[4] All social and moral choice is subsumed within the category of the domestic, suggesting not only that family integrity transcends politics but also that collective affiliation is reducible to being nice to other people—especially relatives. Even *Family Ties*, its white obverse, whose premise of ex-hippie parents with a precorporate, neoconservative son promises some energizing friction, smoothes genuine argument into the cozy warmth of domestic affection. The mild-mannered Keaton father Stephen is persuaded by an old friend from the campus left to restart a radical magazine. A difference of opinion results in Stephen being accused of copping out, but his wife Elyse assures him that "you're making a statement by the way you live your life and raise your children."

Bill Cosby, whose diploma in education is always prominently featured in his show's credits, takes his responsibilities as an educator very seriously. *Newsweek* reported in 1984 that Cosby had commissioned black psychiatrist Alvin Poussaint to review every *Cosby Show* script for "authenticity." The actor told the *Los Angeles Times* in 1985 that viewers loved the series because it showed that "the people in this house respect the parents and the parents respect the children and that there is a l-o-v-e generated in this house." Norman Lear, in his time, felt convinced that viewers liked *All in the Family* not only because it was funny or endearing but because it exposed bigotry and addressed topical issues. There is always a potential asymmetry between producers' intentions and viewers' readings. As I argued in Chapter 4, Bunker fans may just as plausibly have identified with the diffuse rage that imprinted itself on almost every episode of *All in the Family* as with its liberal political stance.[5]

Similarly, the Huxtable brand of patriarchal dominance may strike as resonant a chord as the l-o-v-e Cosby cited—to which the success of his book *Fatherhood*, which topped the bestseller list in 1986, may testify. And if Cosby's childlike charm also works, this dualism in him and in *The Cosby Show* narrative may cater to what is most childlike in his viewers—namely, the yearning (all the more powerful because for many Americans it seems to go unfulfilled) for a perfectly synchronized family or community that provides for the needs of all its members and regulates itself through a benevolent dictatorship. The show's endless rehearsal and efficient mopping up of mild domestic disorder stakes a claim for a perfect family that works, but its closure of all open endings, relative viewpoints, and ethical ambiguities and its energetic repression of the sources of suffering that afflict many families (especially black families) suggest a political retrenchment born of cultural exhaustion, a fearful inability to confront current reality and imagine new forms of community or new ways of living. Both form and meaning work in *The Cosby Show* to obliterate the indeterminacies that emerged in family comedy in the 1970s and to supersede the diversity of family forms in other contemporary series, at the same time binding the interpretive imagination of the viewer.

The aggressive reinstatement of the nuclear family in both television and public discourse, together with the eagerness of programmers to cater to children and teenagers, may account for the decline in workplace comedies, especially during family viewing hours.[6] Workplace dramas, by contrast, abound. The modest ratings success, but rapturous critical and industry acclaim, that attached to NBC's *Hill Street Blues* and CBS's *Cagney and Lacey*, both police dramas, fostered the emergence of other workplace dramatic series, such as *St. Elsewhere* (a run-down hospital), *Moonlighting* (a detective agency with few clients), and *L.A. Law* (a show set in a Los Angeles law firm, in whose members the mixture of frank, materialistic careerism and anxious self-doubt lies at the root of that ambivalent term *yuppie*). All retain some of the familial closeness of the television workplace, but the ensemble grows in size, turning the work-families into loose clans based more on shifting, uneasy alliances than were the tight, small groups of the 1970s shows. This arrangement is clearest in *Hill Street Blues*, whose large cast of morally and psychologically ambiguous characters, along with convoluted, often unresolved story lines running across several episodes, "decenters" the show. The use of hand-held cameras presents viewers with multiple, shifting viewpoints and serves to blur the divisions between the precinct and the outside world. Thus the hectic untidiness of this series and others like it evokes a workplace under siege not only from the terrifying chaos of the inner city but also from its own organizational environment.[7] Chief Daniels in *Hill Street Blues*, Inspector Knelman in *Cagney and Lacey*, and the remote corporate types who want to sell the hospital in *St. Elsewhere* all represent an intensification of that crisis of belief in the integrity and authority of the corporate state and its representatives that marked the workplace of the 1970s. The "good" professional has become one who, like the tight-lipped, beleaguered Captain Furillo in *Hill Street Blues*, can hold the fort against the forces of anarchy and corruption for another day.

In the 1980s, then, the domestic series evacuate the outside world altogether, filling it with nameless fear, or retreat into fundamentalist principles of family, whose rigidity suggests not so much the relaxed confidence born of stability as the fear of total disintegration from within or invasion from without. In the workplace dramas the distinctions between private and public spheres become even more tenuous than they were in the shows of the 1970s. The work-family becomes a more troubled haven, fending off a thoroughly compromised institutional world and set against the background of a decaying and lawless city. The lack of a coherent public world is underscored by the relative absence of the debates about race, class, gender, and generation that, however partial, animated the shows of the 1970s.[8] Into this political vacuum—the family divorced from public life and the workplace threatened by it—slips the breezy vigilantism of series like *The A-Team*, the return of the maverick private investigator (*Magnum P.I.*), and made for TV movies like *The Burning Bed* that glorify desperate individuals who, having been failed by the justice or welfare systems, take matters into their own hands.

Since the early 1970s a dualism has developed in the thinking and practice of those who make and sell television. On the one hand, industry rhetoric stresses the importance of "demographics," the effort to make and schedule "quality" programs for target audiences whose purchasing power and life-style will be attractive to advertisers even though they comprise a smaller audience. On the other hand, the mass audience remains a pertinent category for network programmers, who must still demonstrate (through ratings) to sponsors that their shows draw vast numbers of viewers.[9] Indeed that need grows more urgent as the challenge from pay and cable television, syndicated programming, and home video technology grows stronger since the networks must prove their worth on the basis of crude numbers, in contrast with the more specialized appeal of their competitors.[10] But the dualism, as I argued in Chapter 3, also has a broader social base; the mass audience exists largely as a construct in the minds of those who make and sell television. The heterogeneity of viewers must be simultaneously catered to with pluralistic images and glossed over with a more universal language in order to *create* a mass audience. In the 1970s, I suggested, "relevance" was acceptable because it was framed in a universal institution, the family. The "family pluralism" suggested by the episodic series in the 1980s is weak and tentative, acknowledging more the *variety* of family forms than the *struggle* over meanings of family at the level of gender, race, class, and generation and at the intersection of family with the public world of work. Moreover, family pluralism exists in tension with, and may be contained by, the more monolithic forms and meanings of the top-rated family shows, which insist on a rigidly revisionist interpretation of family life.

In each successive television era a particular congruence of marketing exigencies and cultural trends has produced different portraits of American social life. In network television genre is always about 80 percent commerce. But in the 1970s commercial imperatives made room for lively, innovative programming that interrupted the hitherto bland conventions of the television family, giving us programming that above all did not condescend to its audiences. The Bunkers were never a restful or reassuring family, but their battles, however strident, raised the possibility that there might be—might *have* to be—more ways than one to conduct family life, that blood ties are not the only bonds of community, that divorce is a feature of modern life to be confronted, and that men and women must find new ways of living together and raising children.

In the 1980s too the plurality of form and meaning and the relativistic sensibility of the "dramadies" offer the alarming but challenging proposition that for many Americans in the 1980s, the damaged boundaries of family, love, and work have rendered the texture of modern life so fluid that it becomes not merely uncontrollable but incomprehensible. This proposition has to be confronted, and it is the kind of critical commentary that good storytelling can always provide. The television series did, for a while, provide it, and still does here and there.[11] At its best, television sets up a public argument about volatile matters that resonate deeply with audiences and even threaten to divide them. At its worst, the medium cranks out a pedestrian supply of toothless sermonizing.

In the late 1980s the generous space that was opened up in the 1970s for public discussion is once again being narrowed. With their eyes firmly fixed on the new mass audience (especially its children), *The Cosby Show* and its imitators threaten to quash the quarrelsome liveliness of the shows of the 1970s and the healthy diversity of 1980s television families by burying their heads in the nostalgic sands of "traditional values" that never were. Many family-oriented public interest groups are pleased with the domestic harmony they see in some current entertainment programming, but the obsession with engineering a spurious consensus returns us to the flattest kind of television with its twin besetting sins, sentimentality and a profound horror of argument. For the most part the way the industry works sets limits on the articulation of ambiguity, uncertainty, and the dissident voice. As long as television producers continue to be rewarded for seeing their viewers as markets, they will continue to crank out sentimentally idealized families or "human-condition" shows about "relevant" problems the viewers can weep over, and move on. Over and over, the narratives of television tell us that we are all brothers and sisters under the skin. But it is the social divisions outside the skin that need the public ventilation that television could be giving them but only occasionally does.

Notes

1. Introduction:
Cultural Analysis and Social Change

1. See, for example, Schorske 1980 and Lears 1981 for different analyses of the character and evolution of modernist culture.

2. For an analytical review of United States Census data on marriage and family between 1970 and 1980, see Hacker 1982.

3. See, for example, Rubin 1976 and Sennett and Cobb 1972. One well-publicized exception was the replication of the Lynds' Middletown study (Bahr 1980).

4. See, for example, the critical essay on the work of Lasch and the "new family history" by Breines, Cerullo, and Stacey (1978).

5. See, for example, *Work in America*, the 1978 report of a special task force to the Secretary of Health, Education, and Welfare. For more critical and theoretical analyses, see Aronowitz 1973, Braverman 1974, Edwards 1979, and Garson 1976.

6. See Kanter's *Men and Women of the Corporation* (1977a) and Arlie Hochschild's *The Managed Heart* (1983), a study of flight attendants that shows how women's emotional skills are colonized and transformed into a commercial asset for employers in the workplace.

7. Raymond Williams (1977) and Christopher Lasch (1977) have useful discussions of state and corporate invasion into the private sphere.

8. This is not to say that blue-collar and routine white-collar workers do not search for meaning in their work. Barbara Garson's (1976) observations in a variety of settings show clearly that people doing routine jobs go to great and sometimes bizarre lengths to infuse monotonous work with meaning and creativity.

9. A variety of perspectives on the rise of the professional-managerial

class is offered in *The New Class*, a collection of essays edited by B. Bruce-Briggs (1981).

10. See, for example, Bell 1976, Jacoby 1975, Lasch 1979, Nisbet 1969, and Sennett 1977.

2. Television as Family:
The Episodic Series, 1946–1969

1. Feuer (1987) argues that television genres may be understood respectively as ritual (organizational) categories, aesthetic categories (texts fulfilling canons of artistic expression), or ideological categories (instruments of social control in which dominant ideologies are reproduced). These categories are clearly interrelated, but in television it is useful to begin with the ritual aspect, the exchange between industry and audience, which is paramount.

2. On the political economy of American media industries, see Bagdikian 1983, Barnouw 1975, Czitrom 1982, Monaco 1981, and Williams 1974.

3. The Federal Communications Commission has, to varying degrees over time, proved itself a weak regulatory agency in this sphere, and noncommercial public television commands only a tiny segment of the viewing audience.

4. For a critical discussion of the ways in which mass communicators use the Nielsen ratings, see Gitlin 1985, chapter 3.

5. Stars tend to merge more with the characters they play in television than in other media such as film or theater. Sometimes they even use the same names (Lucille Ball as Lucy Ricardo in *The Lucy Show*, Mary Tyler Moore as Mary Richards in *The Mary Tyler Moore Show*). Accordingly, the off-screen reputations of television stars, at least of those whose shows play in prime time, are generally less flamboyant, more domestic, and more respectable than those of movie stars. With the exception of nighttime soap stars like Joan Collins, who violates all kinds of norms both on and off the screen, few television stars like to acquire a name for wild living or frequent changes of partners, which would damage their credibility as the reassuring familial figures they play. Many do highly publicized charity work in areas that do not require them to take clear political positions on divisive issues. A controversial exception was Ed Asner, whose off-screen activities appeared to extend the populist advocacy of *Lou Grant* to the point where the actor became unacceptable, if not to viewers, then to sponsors and network executives. See the discussion of *Lou Grant* in Gitlin 1985, 3–11.

6. Students who watch reruns of *Father Knows Best* in my classes roar

with derisive laughter when Margaret Anderson, surprised by her husband's early return from the office, panics at being caught in the clothes she wears for housework. Yet they also seem to love the reassuring stability of the Andersons' calm lives.

7. By the late 1970s the earnest solemnity of *Dragnet* and its heroes' inevitable victories had become so implausible that it provided ripe material for lampooning in comedies, satirical shows, and even commercials.

8. Mick Eaton (1978) argues in his critique of the television sitcom that "both the past and the future articulate with the present of television viewing in terms of the former being 'just like now but less so' and the latter 'just like now but more so' " (72).

3. Prime-Time Relevance:
Television Entertainment Programming
in the 1970s

1. See, for example, Roszak 1969 and Reich 1971.

2. For an account of this process in media coverage of the 1960s antiwar movement, see Gitlin 1980.

3. My discussion of the rise of "relevant" programming in television entertainment draws substantially on Gitlin 1985, chapter 10.

4. The slow climb to success of *All in the Family* and other shows of its kind taught programming executives an important lesson from which innovative series such as *Hill Street Blues* would later benefit, namely, that some series, especially those that are dependent on the development of character and ensemble, pick up audience loyalty only slowly and must be given time to "take" with viewers.

5. Both the National Council for Families and Television and Action for Children's Television, for example, engage in strenuous efforts to influence the thinking of television producers, as do religious groups such as Donald Wildmon's Coalition for Better Television.

6. The history of television is also littered with failed attempts to second-guess cultural trends and cash in on them. See, for example, Gitlin's (1985) account of the failure of several new espionage and adventure shows to appeal to a presumed shift to the right among viewers in the 1981 season (chapter 11). I discuss this matter further in Chapter 6.

7. Almost none of the successful producers of "relevant" series during this period were baby boomers; most were considerably older. Some of the writers, however, who began their careers working for Tandem or MTM and went on to become successful writer-producers in the 1980s belonged to the "sixties generation." Gary David Goldberg, for example,

now the executive producer of Ubu Productions, was a 1965 Brandeis University dropout who worked on the first *Bob Newhart Show* and on *Lou Grant* before making the highly successful *Family Ties*.

8. Larry Gelbart, producer of *M*A*S*H*, blamed the shoddiness of much television entertainment on the "hand-to-mouth, let's-have-it-yesterday atmosphere that often bedevils producers of prime time series in this country" (*New York Times*, March 9, 1980). David Levy, a former NBC vice-president turned producer, was more circumspect: "We're not so militant that we would destroy the [network] system that has made our lives possible. But . . . this madness that drives the network, this drive to win every half hour time period, results in mediocrity. If a program does not appeal to the 18 to 49 year old housewife, its chances of getting on network television are very slim" (quoted in Paul Bernstein, "Producers Are Mad as Hell and They Aren't Going to Take It Any More," *Passages*, March 1980, 20–23).

9. Data that suggest viewers are not watching when the television set is on, or that they are using videocassette recorders to zap through commercials or watch at their own convenience, are unlikely to meet with a warm welcome in network research units. This in part accounts for the resistance by networks to the Nielsen companies' switch to "people meters," which try to approximate more closely *how* people watch television.

10. Hartley 1984 has a useful discussion of how the family, which in television is at once fundamental and taken for granted, is, to use Roland Barthes' (1981) term, "ex-nominated" or rendered natural. Fiske and Hartley (1978) argue that television "claws back" marginal or oppositional meanings into a consensual center.

11. See, for example, Hartley 1984, Johnson 1986–1987, Long 1986, Radway 1987, and Schudson 1987. For empirical studies of audience interaction with media, see Katz and Liebes 1986, Lull 1980, Radway 1984, and the work of the Birmingham school in Hall et al. 1980.

12. In the prodigious body of work he amassed from 1958 until his death in 1988, Raymond Williams conducted a long examination of the meaning and origins of culture. His insistence on grasping culture as *social practice* has provided the solid ground on which much of the theoretical and empirical work of the developing interdisciplinary tradition of cultural studies (especially the work of the Birmingham school and the Centre for Mass Communication Research at Leicester University in England) rests, and has exercised a profound influence on my own research. See Hall et al. 1980 for an account of the work of the Birmingham school, Johnson 1986–1987 for a critical discussion of current

developments in cultural studies, and Carey 1983 for an analysis of the development of cultural studies in the United States.

13. My own reading of the meanings of television is rooted in the shift from content analysis and effects research to the developing theory of language and ideology, which in its various forms sees the text not as reflection but as mediation of the real through the activity of language. Taken together, the contributions of phenomenology, structuralism, its subfield semiotics, and its successor poststructuralism have adopted the refusal of obvious meaning as the central project of interpretive work (Hall et al. 1980, Johnson 1986–1987). The language of a text neither reflects nor precisely distorts lived experience; it produces messages that provide a commentary on "the real." Meaning thus becomes encoded in the next through processes of signification that occur in the work of production and reception (Hall 1980).

According to this view, meaning is construed not as a fixed message lying immanent within the text but as a whole range of shifting, multiple meanings that are filtered and constituted through language and context. The interpreter's task is to try to grasp the flow of social discourse and, as Geertz (1973) puts it, "rescue the 'said' of such discourse from its perishing occasions and fix it in perusable terms" (20). The possible readings of television may be many, but they are neither infinite nor arbitrary. Poststructuralist and deconstructionist theories introduce an appropriate relativism into the study of modern cultural forms, whose meanings are nothing if not ambiguous; but they also carry the potential danger of silencing cultural critique altogether. That is to say, without the concrete historical analysis of institutions and forms one can deconstruct oneself into a position in which nothing valid can be said about anything at all. If a television show engages the sustained attention of its viewers, it is speaking to events and experiences that matter to them in ways with which they can identify. The longevity of $M^*A^*S^*H$ may derive from good acting and lively scriptwriting, from the resonance of its antiwar sensibility for the post–Vietnam War generation, from the appeal of its adolescent prankishness for younger viewers, or from other factors not considered here.

More generally, television representations of work and family *produce ideas* about family and work within the conventions of the medium. Like other forms of popular culture, the television narrative remaps the social world, reflecting received conventions, articulating their contradictions, and prefiguring new values. The major part of my project is to uncover the rules that structure this selectivity and to clarify some of its meanings. Situating my investigation in the twin principles of television as social practice and as relatively autonomous text, I have moved between close observation of the recurring internal detail of television texts and a grounding of that detail in the larger symbolic world of the television narrative, the conditions of its production and reception, and the social world it inhabits and tries to explain to itself.

14. Within the category of episodic series with family or workplace settings, shows were selected for intensive analysis if they met one or more of the following criteria: (1) Shows were included if they entered the top twenty in the Nielsen ratings for at least one season. As the discussion in Chapter 2 shows, ratings are at best a rough index, not of audience taste, but of viewers' choices within the narrow range of the entertainment fare they are offered. Ratings are important because producers, network executives, and advertisers act on them; in this sense they influence both industry policy and the form of the shows produced. (2) Some series (*Barney Miller, Taxi, Lou Grant*) did not achieve a sustained or even fleeting presence in the top twenty but are significant because they attracted a substantial and loyal following over several seasons, enjoyed long runs in syndication, exemplified the house style of a particular production company, or were innovative in modifying genre forms and conventions (*Mary Hartman, Mary Hartman*).

A minimum of ten episodes was analyzed in detail. Series that broke with the "relevance" doctrine after 1975 (ABC hits such as *Happy Days* and *Mork and Mindy*) and those that had less direct bearing on the work and family themes (*The Rockford Files*) were examined in less depth in order to provide an overall picture of prime-time entertainment programming in the 1970s.

4. Trouble at Home:
Television's Changing Families, 1970–1980

1. Michael Arlen (1976), television critic for *The New Yorker*, estimated that early in the series 120 million Americans watched *All in the Family* each week and 5 billion each year.

2. CBS News, commenting in 1984 on Walter Mondale's choice of Geraldine Ferraro as running mate and Democratic vice-presidential candidate, described Ferraro as coming from "an Archie Bunker neighborhood"—an index of her popularity with blue-collar voters.

3. My own experience in discussing *All in the Family* with undergraduate students in Massachusetts, California, and Washington confirms this pattern of response.

4. Throughout the latter part of the 1970s Lear was becoming more active in political life (at the same time as his comedies were growing less overtly political.) In 1978 he left active television production and in 1980

founded People for the American Way, an organization devoted to opposing the New Right.

5. Esther Rolle and John Amos left the cast of *Good Times* in protest against its crude characterizations, especially in the character of J. J., who had become something of a cult figure among young viewers and whom Rolle in particular considered a poor role model for black children.

6. The bereaved state persists through the 1970s and 1980s, principally for male leads in dramatic series like *Quincy, Marcus Welby,* and *St. Elsewhere* (Dr. Westphall), as a handy but unchallenging device for freeing a caring professional to dedicate himself to his work and his clients while maintaining his credibility as a moral and professional role model.

7. This is an obvious dig by the producers at the inaccuracies of the ratings system, but it also proposes the family as a lunatic asylum.

8. See Janice Radway 1984 on romance novels and Tania Modleski 1979 on daytime soap operas.

5. All in the Work-Family: Television Families in Workplace Settings

1. In the 1980s, shows that sought to depict the lives of routine workers, such as *Skag* (a series about the steel industry), *Making a Living* (about waitressing), and *Nine to Five* (a movie spin-off about routine clerical work), met with little success in the ratings and were quickly canceled by the networks.

2. See my discussion of Brooks's comments in Chapter 3.

3. Brooks and Burns had intended Mary to be a divorcée, but CBS vetoed this idea, insisting that audiences were not ready for it (Gitlin 1985, 214).

4. The image of the incomplete woman is by no means new in contemporary popular culture. As Andrea Walsh (1984) shows, the Hollywood films of the 1940s abound with images of women coping alone. The difference is that in the films of the 1940s men are often absent; in the TV series of the 1970s men are present but are inadequate to their women or unwilling to commit themselves to permanent partnerships.

5. Despite the popularity of *M*A*S*H* and the spectacular ratings that attended its final episode in 1983, its spin-off, *Aftermash,* which relocated some of the original cast in a hospital back in the United States, was an almost immediate flop.

6. In its later seasons *Lou Grant* becomes both more open-ended in its narrative structure and more docudramatic, sometimes basing story lines on current events or social issues such as toxic-waste dumping. In this way

the series comes to resemble, rather than resolve, the ambiguities of everyday life. It thus becomes didactic without also being redemptive, which may account in part for its falling ratings.

7. Significantly, Dr. Welby returned in the 1980s in a made-for-TV movie as a hospital employee threatened with layoff when budget cuts compel his employers to trim the staff, beginning with older employees.

8. In many of these shows a good deal of hostility is displayed toward technology itself. In *Barney Miller*, for example, viewers' sympathies are directed toward a man who is arrested for assaulting a malfunctioning candy machine; and Dietrich outwits a "stress-testing" computer, attached to him by an outside expert, for measuring levels of stress in police work.

6. Family Television Then and Now

1. David Poltrack, vice-president of marketing for CBS, remarked in an interview with *TV Guide* (July 23, 1988) that it is children and teens who switch on the television set between 8 and 9 P.M.: "They are the ones getting the set turned on, they are building the audience. *But* we sell adults to advertisers in prime time, so if we can also have empathetic adults for the parents to relate to, they will join to watch *with* the child" (8).

2. The power of the lineup is illustrated by the success of the *Cosby Show* spinoff *A Different World*, which was widely panned by critics but has been carried in the ratings by its position immediately following *The Cosby Show*.

3. NBC's *Cosby Show* was paired with the only marginally less successful *Family Ties*, and their joint popularity no doubt inspired ABC's *Growing Pains* and *Valerie*, both series about intact nuclear families.

4. For a useful discussion of the newer "black shows," see Herman Gray 1986.

5. At this point one needs to know more about viewers' interactions with television. I have argued that television audiences are more aware of genre distinctions and conventions than are audiences for other aesthetic forms, but it is far from clear what they do with these distinctions. Is the regulative force of genre in television, its power to shape and limit the construction of meaning in the text and in viewers, dissolving? Do viewers still draw boundaries between comedies and dramatic series and between the series and the serial, or do they respond to strips of viewing or, more broadly, to the flow of television programming? Do they relate to

television families as approximations of real-life families? Can we assume that the most popular shows perpetuate dominant ideas *for viewers?* Years of discussing television with college students at both the undergraduate and graduate levels lead me to the conclusion that they at least have rather complex attitudes toward television. In the nervous laughter or skeptically raised eyebrows I see when I solemnly exhort them to watch television for social-scientific purposes lies at least a partial clue to the public ambivalence that has beset the medium since its infancy. Many of them watch a great deal of television, and they need little prodding to discuss it both in the classroom and outside it. But their viewing and their discussion are colored by the conviction—absorbed from parents, teachers, university professors, and television itself—that at best, television will waste their time, and at worst, it will soften their brains, rendering them passive, desensitized, uneducated, mediocre, or even violent. This ambivalence alone cautions against a simple reading of the relationship between television and its audiences. Genre analysis can point us in the direction of viewers' and producers' constructions of meaning, but a fuller understanding requires an ethnography of audience participation in television as well as an account of the work of television production. See Radway 1987 and Schudson 1987.

6. NBC's *Cheers* and *Night Court* and CBS's *Murphy Brown* endure, but they are 1970s-style work-families very much in the MTM mold.

7. There is a marked resemblance in theme and form between shows like *Hill Street Blues* and movies like *Prince of the City* and *Fort Apache, the Bronx*. The capacity of the small screen to accommodate the busy chaos of urban life is stretched to the limit in *Hill Street Blues*; one of my colleagues complained that the series was "too cubist" for him to watch.

8. A Johannesburg television executive, asked on the Hollywood chat show *Entertainment Tonight* why he thought *The Cosby Show* was number one in the South African ratings, observed complacently but correctly that the show was not about race but about "family values."

9. Brandon Tartikoff, NBC's president of entertainment, observed that although the 75 million baby-boomer viewers were the biggest prize in terms of ratings, "we are in the business of trying to achieve a mass audience whenever we can" (*New York Times*, October 30, 1988, Arts and Leisure section, 28). For the networks, the optimal goal is to reach both audiences with one show or one evening lineup. Said Tartikoff: "I sat in a theater in Los Angeles on a Saturday afternoon and saw *Babyboom*, and I was probably the youngest moviegoer in the room. The *Love Boat* crowd was all around me. I thought, here's something about a person in the 35–49-year-old age group, with a kid, and the *Love Boat* crowd is loving

it. Obviously, it was broader than *Thirtysomething*" (ibid.). NBC promptly developed a series modeled after *Babyboom* for its fall 1988 season.

10. "The one thing that the audience is, more than ever, is fickle," remarked Ted Harbert, vice-president for prime-time entertainment at ABC. "It is harder and harder to get them to sit down and watch an entire night of ABC programs" (ibid.).

11. *The Days and Nights of Molly Dodd, The Wonder Years,* and *Murphy Brown,* for example, offer both the crisp scriptwriting and the critical edge that characterized television comedy in the 1970s.

Bibliography

Arlen, Michael. 1982. *Living Room War*. New York: Penguin Books.

_____. 1976. "The Media Dramas of Norman Lear." In Michael Arlen, *The View from Highway One: Essays on Television*, 53–66. New York: Farrar, Straus and Giroux.

Aronowitz, Stanley. 1973. *False Promises: The Shaping of American Class Consciousness*. New York: McGraw-Hill.

Bagdikian, Ben. 1983. *The Media Monopoly*. Boston: Beacon Press.

Bahr, Howard. 1980. "Changes in Family Life in Middletown, 1924–77." *Public Opinion Quarterly* 44, no. 1 (Spring): 35–52.

Bane, Mary Jo. 1976. *Here to Stay: American Families in the Twentieth Century*. New York: Basic Books.

Barnouw, Erik. 1978. *The Sponsor: Notes on a Modern Potentate*. New York: Oxford University Press.

_____. 1975. *Tube of Plenty: The Evolution of American Television*. New York: Oxford University Press.

Barthes, Roland. 1981. "Theory of the Text." In *Untying the Text: A Post-Structuralist Reader*, edited by Robert Young. London: Routledge and Kegan Paul.

Bathrick, Serafina. 1984. "*The Mary Tyler Moore Show*: Women at Home and at Work." In *MTM "Quality Television*," edited by Jane Feuer, Paul Kerr, and Tise Vahimagi, 99–131. London: British Film Institute.

Bell, Daniel. 1976. *The Cultural Contradictions of Capitalism*. New York: Basic Books.

Bellah, Robert N., Richard Madsen, William M. Sullivan, Ann Swidler, and Steven Tipton. 1985. *Habits of the Heart: Individualism and Commitment in American Life*. Berkeley: University of California Press.

Berman, Marshall. 1982. *All That Is Solid Melts into Air: The Experience of Modernity*. New York: Simon and Schuster.

Braverman, Harry. 1974. *Labor and Monopoly Capital: The Degradation of Work in the Twentieth Century*. New York: Monthly Review Press.

Breines, Wini, Margaret Cerullo, and Judith Stacey. 1978. "Social Biology, Family Studies, and Anti-Feminist Backlash." *Feminist Studies* 4, no. 1:43–67.

Brooks, Tim, and Earle Marsh. 1985. *The Complete Directory to Prime Time Network TV Shows 1946–Present*. New York: Ballantine Books.

Bruce-Briggs, B. 1981. *The New Class*. New York: McGraw-Hill.

Cantor, Muriel. 1980. *Prime Time Television: Content and Control*. Beverly Hills: Sage.

Carey, James W. 1983. "The Origins of the Radical Discourse on Cultural Studies in the United States." *Journal of Communication* 33, no. 3 (Summer): 311–313.

Castleman, Harry, and Walter J. Podrazik. 1982. *Watching TV: Four Decades of American Television*. New York: McGraw-Hill.

Cawelti, John. 1976. *Adventure, Mystery, and Romance: Formula Stories as Art and Popular Culture*. Chicago: University of Chicago Press.

Czitrom, Daniel. 1982. *Media and the American Mind: From Morse to McLuhan*. Chapel Hill: University of North Carolina Press.

Durkheim, Emile. 1964. *The Division of Labor in Society*. New York: Free Press.

Eagleton, Terry. 1983. *Literary Theory: An Introduction*. Minneapolis: University of Minnesota Press.

Eaton, Mick. 1978–1979. "Television Situation Comedy." *Screen* 19:61–91.

Edwards, Richard. 1979. *Contested Terrain: The Transformation of the American Workplace in the Twentieth Century*. New York: Basic Books.

Ehrenreich, Barbara. 1976. "*Mary Hartman:* A World Out of Control." *Socialist Revolution* 6, no. 4:133–138.

Feuer, Jane. 1987. "Genre Study and Television." In *Channels of Discourse: Television and Contemporary Criticism* ed. Robert C. Allen. Chapel Hill: University of North Carolina Press: 113–133.

Feuer, Jane, Paul Kerr, and Tise Vahimagi, eds. 1984. *MTM "Quality Television."* London: British Film Institute.

Fiske, John. 1987. *Television Culture*. New York: Methuen.

Fiske, John, and John Hartley. 1978. *Reading Television*. London: Methuen.

Gans, Herbert. 1957. "The Creator-Audience Relationship in the Mass Media." In *Mass Culture*, edited by Bernard Rosenberg and David

Manning White, 315–324. New York: Free Press.

————. 1980. *Deciding What's News*. New York: Vintage Books.

Garson, Barbara. 1976. *All the Livelong Day: The Meaning and Demeaning of Routine Work*. New York: Penguin.

Geertz, Clifford. 1973. *The Interpretation of Cultures*. New York: Basic Books.

Giddens, Anthony. 1979. *Central Problems in Social Theory: Action, Structure, and Contradiction in Social Analysis*. Berkeley: University of California Press.

Gitlin, Todd. 1985. *Inside Prime Time*. New York: Pantheon Books.

————. 1978. "Media Sociology: The Dominant Paradigm." *Theory and Society* 6, no. 2:205–253.

————. 1979. "Prime Time Ideology: The Hegemonic Process in Television Entertainment." *Social Problems* 26, no. 3:251–266.

————. 1980. *The Whole World Is Watching: Mass Media in the Making and Unmaking of the New Left*. Berkeley: University of California Press.

————, ed. 1986. *Watching Television*. New York: Pantheon.

Gray, Herman. 1986. "Television and the New Black Man: Black Male Images In Prime-Time Situation Comedy." *Media, Culture and Society* 8, no. 2:223–242.

Hacker, Andrew. 1982. "Farewell to the Family?" *New York Review of Books* 29, no. 4:37–45.

Hall, Stuart. 1980. "Encoding/Decoding." In *Culture, Media, Language*, edited by Stuart Hall, Dorothy Hobson, Andrew Lowe, and Paul Willis, 128–138. London: Hutchinson.

Hall, Stuart, Dorothy Hobson, Andrew Lowe, and Paul Willis, eds. 1980. *Culture, Media, Language*. London: Hutchinson.

Hall, Stuart, and Tony Jefferson, eds. 1976. *Resistance through Rituals: Youth Subcultures in Post War Britain*. London: Hutchinson.

Hardwick, Elizabeth. 1978. "Domestic Manners." *Daedalus* 107, no. 1:6–15.

Hartley, John. 1984. "Encouraging Signs: Television and the Power of Dirt, Speech, and Scandalous Categories." In *Interpreting Television: Current Research Perspectives*, edited by Willard D. Rowland, Jr., and Bruce Watkins, 119–141. Beverly Hills: Sage.

Held, David. 1980. *Introduction to Critical Theory: Horkheimer to Habermas*. Berkeley: University of California Press.

Hochschild, Arlie Russell. 1983. *The Managed Heart: Commercialization of Human Feeling*. Berkeley: University of California Press.

Hodgson, Godfrey. 1976. *America in Our Time*. New York: Vintage Books.

Hunt, Albert. 1981. *The Language of Television: Uses and Abuses*. London: Methuen.

Jacoby, Russell. 1975. *Social Amnesia: A Critique of Contemporary Psychology from Adler to Laing*. Boston: Beacon Press.

Jameson, Fredric. 1977. "Ideology, Narrative Analysis, and Popular Culture." *Theory and Society* 4:543–559.

Johnson, Richard. 1986–1987. "What Is Cultural Studies Anyway?" *Social Text* 6, no. 1 (Winter): 38–80.

Kanter, Rosabeth Moss. 1977a. *Men and Women of the Corporation*. New York: Basic Books.

_____. 1977b. *Work and Family in the United States: A Critical Review and Agenda for Research and Policy*. New York: Russell Sage Foundation.

_____. 1978. "Work in a New America." *Daedalus* 107 (Winter): 47–78.

Katz, Elihu, and Tamar Liebes. 1986. "Mutual Aid in the Decoding of *Dallas*: Preliminary Notes from a Cross-cultural Study." In *Television in Transition*, edited by Phillip Drummond and Richard Peterson, 187–198. London: British Film Institute.

Kermode, Frank. 1986. "Modernisms." *London Review of Books*, May 22, 3–6.

Kerr, Paul. 1984. "The Making of (The) MTM (Show)." In *MTM "Quality Television*," edited by Jane Feuer, Paul Kerr, and Tise Vahimagi, 61–98. London: British Film Institute.

Lasch, Christopher. 1981. "Archie Bunker and the Liberal Mind." *Channels of Communications* (October/November).

_____. 1979. *The Culture of Narcissism: American Life in an Age of Diminishing Expectations*. New York: Warner Books.

_____. 1977. *Haven in a Heartless World: The Family Besieged*. New York: Basic Books.

_____. 1984. *The Minimal Self: Psychic Survival in Troubled Times*. New York: Norton.

Lears, T. Jackson. 1981. *No Place of Grace: Anti-modernism and the Transformation of American Culture 1880–1920*. New York: Pantheon Books.

Leinberger, Paul. 1986. " 'Organization Man' Revisited." *The New York Times Magazine*, 7 December.

Long, Elizabeth. 1985. *The American Dream and the Popular Novel*. Boston: Routledge and Kegan Paul.

_____. 1986. "Women, Reading and Cultural Authority." *American Quarterly* 38, no. 4:591–610.

Lull, James T. 1980. "Family Communication Patterns and the Social Uses of Television." *Communications Research* 7, no. 3:319–334.

Maccoby, Michael. 1976. *The Gamesman*. New York: Simon and Schuster.

Marc, David. 1984. *Demographic Vistas: Television in American Culture*. Philadelphia: University of Pennsylvania Press.

Meyer, Timothy P. 1976. "The Impact of *All in the Family* on Children." *Journal of Broadcasting* 20:23–33.

Modleski, Tania. 1980. "The Disappearing Act: A Study of Harlequin Romances." *Signs* 5 (Spring): 435–448.

_____. 1979. "The Search for Tomorrow in Today's Soap Operas: Notes on a Feminine Narrative Form." *Film Quarterly* 33, no. 1 (Fall): 12–21.

Monaco, James. 1981. *How to Read a Film*. New York: Oxford University Press.

Morley, David. 1986. *Family Television: Cultural Power and Domestic Leisure*. London: Comedia Publishing Group.

_____. 1980a. *The "Nationwide" Audience*. London: British Film Institute.

_____. 1980b. "Texts, Readers, Subjects." In *Culture, Media, Language*, edited by Stuart Hall, Dorothy Hobson, Andrew Lowe, and Paul Willis, 163–173. London: Hutchinson.

Murdock, Graham, and Peter Golding. 1977. "Capitalism, Communication, and Class Relations." In *Mass Communication and Society*, edited by James Curran, Michael Gurevitch, and Janet Woollacott, 12–43. London: Edward Arnold.

Newcomb, Horace. 1984. "On the Dialogic Aspects of Mass Communication." *Critical Studies in Mass Communication* 1, no. 1:34–50.

_____. 1974. *TV. The Most Popular Art*. Garden City: Anchor Press.

Newcomb, Horace, and Robert S. Alley. 1983. *The Producer's Medium: Conversations with Creators of American Television*. New York: Oxford University Press.

Newcomb, Horace, and Paul S. Hirsch. 1984. "Television as a Cultural Forum: Implications for Research." In *Interpreting Television*, edited by Willard Rowland and Bruce Watkins, 58–73. Beverly Hills: Sage.

Nisbet, Robert. 1969. *The Quest for Community*. New York: Oxford University Press.

Radway, Janice. 1984. *Reading the Romance: Women, Patriarchy, and Popular Literature*. Chapel Hill: University of North Carolina Press.

_____. 1987. "Where is 'the Field?': Ethnography, Audiences and the Redesign of Research Practice." Paper delivered at the annual meetings of the International Communications Association, Montreal.

Reich, Charles. 1971. *The Greening of America*. New York: Bantam Books.

Rieff, Philip. 1968. *The Triumph of the Therapeutic: Uses of Faith after Freud*. New York: Harper & Row.

Roszak, Theodore. 1969. *The Making of a Counterculture: Reflections on the Technological Society and Its Youthful Opposition*. New York: Doubleday.

Rubin, Lillian Breslow. 1976. *Worlds of Pain: Life in the Working-Class Family*. New York: Basic Books.

Schorske, Carl. 1980. *Fin-de-Siecle Vienna: Politics and Culture*. New York: Knopf.

Schudson, Michael. 1984. *Advertising: the Uneasy Persuasion*. New York: Basic Books.

———. 1987. "The New Validation of Popular Culture: Sense and Sentimentality in Academia." *Critical Studies in Mass Communication* 4 (March): 51–68.

Sennett, Richard. 1977. *The Fall of Public Man: On the Social Psychology of Capitalism*. New York: Knopf.

Sennett, Richard, and Jonathan Cobb. 1972. *The Hidden Injuries of Class*. New York: Vintage Books.

Shorter, Edward. 1975. *The Making of the Modern Family*. New York: Basic Books.

Slater, Philip. 1970. *The Pursuit of Loneliness: American Culture at the Breaking Point*. Boston: Beacon Press.

Snitow, Ann Barr. 1979. "Mass Market Romance: Pornography for Women Is Different." *Radical History Review* 20 (Spring/Summer): 141–161.

Stack, Carol. 1974. *All Our Kin: Strategies for Survival in a Black Community*. New York: Harper & Row.

Talbot, David, and Barbara Zheutlin. 1978. *Creative Differences: Profiles of Hollywood Dissidents*. Boston: South End Press.

Taylor, Ella. 1988. "Forget Murder and Car Chases: Now It's 'Slice of Life' Shows." *New York Times,* 17 April, Arts and Leisure section.

———. 1987. "TV Dramas: Sweet Agreement, Little Grit." *New York Times,* 16 August, Arts and Leisure section.

———. 1987. "TV Families." *Boston Review* 12; no. 5 (October).

Taylor, Ella, and Andrea S. Walsh. 1987. " 'And Next Week—Child Abuse': Family Issues in Contemporary TV Movies." In *Culture and Communication—Methodology, Behavior, Artifacts and Institutions,* edited by Sari Thomas, 168–177. New Jersey: Ablex.

Tuchman, Gaye. 1978. *Making News: A Study in the Construction of Reality*. New York: Free Press.

Vidmar, Neil, and Milton Rokeach. 1974. "Archie Bunker's Bigotry: A

Study in Selective Perception and Exposure." *Journal of Communication* 24, no. 1:36–47.

Walsh, Andrea S. 1984. *Women's Film and Female Experience*. New York: Praeger.

Warshow, Robert. 1979. *The Immediate Experience: Movies, Comics, Theater and Other Aspects of Popular Culture*. New York: Atheneum.

Williams, Raymond. 1975. *The Country and the City*. London: Paladin.

_____. 1958. *Culture and Society 1780–1950*. London: Chatto and Windus.

_____. 1961. *The Long Revolution*. London: Chatto and Windus.

_____. 1977. *Marxism and Literature*. London: Oxford University Press.

_____. 1974. *Television: Technology and Cultural Form*. London: Fontana.

Willis, Ellen. 1982. "The Family: Love It or Leave It." In Ellen Willis, *Beginning to See the Light: Pieces of a Decade*, 149–168. New York: Widcview Books.

Wolf, M., T. Meyer, and C. White. 1982. "A Rules-Based Study of Television's Role in the Construction of Social Reality." *Journal of Broadcasting* 26, no. 4:813–829.

Work in America: Report of a Special Task Force to the Secretary of Health, Education and Welfare. 1973. Boston: MIT Press.

Wright, Will. 1975. *Sixguns and Society: A Structural Study of the Western*. Berkeley: University of California Press.

Index

Compositor: Interactive Composition Corporation
Text: 11/13 Caledonia
Display: Caledonia
Printer: Edwards Brothers, Inc.
Binder: Edwards Brothers, Inc.